The American

Books on the Civil War Era

Steven E. Woodworth, Associate Professor of History,
Texas Christian University
SERIES EDITOR

~∽∕ The Civil War was the crisis of the Republic's first century
—the test, in Abraham Lincoln's words, of whether any free government could long endure. It touched with fire the hearts of a generation, and its story has fired the imaginations of every generation since.
This series offers to students of the Civil War, either those continuing
or those just beginning their exciting journey into the past, concise
overviews of important persons, events, and themes in that remarkable
period of America's history.

Volumes Published

James L. Abrahamson. *The Men of Secession and Civil War, 1859–1861*
(2000). Cloth ISBN 0-8420-2818-8   Paper ISBN 0-8420-2819-6

Robert G. Tanner. *Retreat to Victory? Confederate Strategy Reconsidered*
(2001). Cloth ISBN 0-8420-2881-1   Paper ISBN 0-8420-2882-X

Stephen Davis. *Atlanta Will Fall: Sherman, Joe Johnston, and the Yankee
Heavy Battalions* (2001). Cloth ISBN 0-8420-2787-4
Paper ISBN 0-8420-2788-2

Paul Ashdown and Edward Caudill. *The Mosby Myth: A Confederate
Hero in Life and Legend* (2002). Cloth ISBN 0-8420-2928-1   Paper
ISBN 0-8420-2929-X

Spencer C. Tucker. *A Short History of the Civil War at Sea* (2002). Cloth
ISBN 0-8420-2867-6   Paper ISBN 0-8420-2868-4

Richard Bruce Winders. *Crisis in the Southwest: The United States,
Mexico, and the Struggle over Texas* (2002). Cloth ISBN 0-8420-
2800-5   Paper ISBN 0-8420-2801-3

Ethan S. Rafuse. *A Single Grand Victory: The First Campaign and Battle
of Manassas* (2002). Cloth ISBN 0-8420-2875-7
Paper ISBN 0-8420-2876-5

John G. Selby. *Virginians at War: The Civil War Experiences of Seven Young Confederates* (2002). Cloth ISBN 0-8420-5054-X Paper ISBN 0-8420-5055-8

Edward K. Spann. *Gotham at War: New York City, 1860–1865* (2002). Cloth ISBN 0-8420-5056-6   Paper ISBN 0-8420-5057-4

Anne J. Bailey. *War and Ruin: William T. Sherman and the Savannah Campaign* (2003). Cloth ISBN 0-8420-2850-1 Paper ISBN 0-8420-2851-X

Gary Dillard Joiner. *One Damn Blunder from Beginning to End: The Red River Campaign of 1864* (2003). Cloth ISBN 0-8420-2936-2 Paper ISBN 0-8420-2937-0

War and Ruin

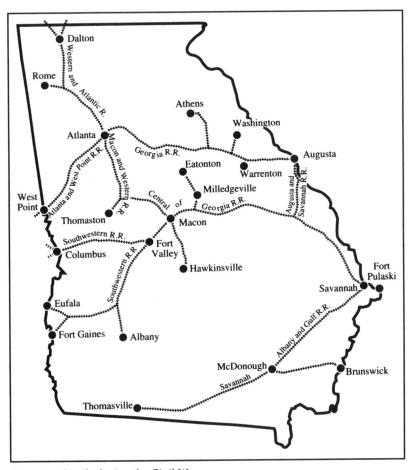

Georgia railroads during the Civil War

War and Ruin
William T. Sherman and the Savannah Campaign

The American Crisis Series
BOOKS ON THE CIVIL WAR ERA
NO. 10

Anne J. Bailey

A Scholarly Resources Inc. Imprint
Wilmington, Delaware

Scholarly Resources Inc.
104 Greenhill Avenue
Wilmington, DE 19805-1897
www.scholarly.com

Library of Congress Cataloging-in-Publication Data

Bailey, Anne J.
  War and ruin : William T. Sherman and the Savannah campaign / Anne J. Bailey.
     p. cm. — (American crisis series ; no. 10)
  Includes bibliographical references (p.) and index.
  ISBN 0-8420-2850-1 (alk. paper) — ISBN 0-8420-2851-X (pbk. : alk. paper)
  1. Savannah (Ga.)—History—Siege, 1864. 2. Sherman, William T. (William Tecumseh), 1820–1891. I. Title. II. Series.

E477.41 .B35 2002
973.7'378—dc21   2002021843

For Grady McWhiney

friend and mentor

About the Author

Anne J. Bailey is a professor of history at Georgia College and State University, the state's public liberal arts institution. She earned her bachelor's from the University of Texas at Arlington and M.A. and Ph.D. from Texas Christian University, where she studied under Grady McWhiney. She is the author of more than 140 articles and reviews and five books on the Civil War; her last two books focused on the Civil War Western Theater. She currently serves as editor of the *Georgia Historical Quarterly*; general editor of "Great Campaigns of the Civil War," a series published by the University of Nebraska Press; and editor of the *SCWH Newsletter*, a quarterly publication of the Society of Civil War Historians. Bailey lives in Milledgeville, Georgia, the state capital during the Civil War.

CONTENTS

INTRODUCTION

WILLIAM TECUMSEH SHERMAN'S Civil War reputation rests less on his accomplishments during the first three years of the war than on the fame he won in the conflict's last eleven months. His capture of Atlanta in September 1864 was timely, both politically and militarily, but it was the march across Georgia in late 1864 and on into South Carolina early in 1865 that burned his name into the annals of history. To Southerners he became an archvillain, a brutal warrior who made war on innocent women, children, and old men. His march to the sea just before Christmas 1864 shocked Southerners more deeply than a battle would have, for people expected carnage and suffering in combat. They did not expect war on a people living in a region that offered no substantial military rewards.

The Atlanta campaign took almost four months, May to September 1864, whereas the Savannah campaign consumed just the four weeks from mid-November to mid-December. But the march across Georgia involved the state's civilian population in a way they had not experienced during the previous three and one-half years of the conflict. After the surrender of Savannah, however, six weeks elapsed before Sherman struck into South Carolina. Since newspapers had reported details of his passage through Georgia, South Carolinians knew what they could expect when the Union columns crossed into their state. As the noted Southern author and South Carolina native William Gilmore Simms had predicted when the Confederate army moved away from Atlanta, "I then declared my opinion that if Sherman had the requisite audacity—it did not need Genius,—he would achieve the greatest of his successes, by turning his back on the enemy in his rear, & march boldly forward towards the Atlantic coast. I fear that such is his purpose. If so,— what have we to oppose him?"[1]

The answer was that the Confederacy had nothing that could stop Sherman. Moreover, for civilians living in central and southeastern Georgia, Sherman's visit was unexpected; they had always believed that the Confederate government would protect their homes from the enemy. Even Confederate president Jefferson Davis had promised not to abandon Georgia.

Sheltered safely in the Lower South, most of Georgia had been spared the devastating ravages of war until Sherman opened his spring campaign in 1864. But for ordinary people in regions where the fighting was intense, the war had brought bewildering societal changes, and in some cases civilians had even become the targets of directed violence. In 1863, Sherman had ordered retribution against families harboring Confederates who fired at shipping on the Mississippi River. In Missouri that same year, the violence against Southern sympathizers reached a peak when Brigadier General Thomas E. Ewing (Sherman's foster brother and brother-in-law) forced the evacuation of some 20,000 people, and almost all of their homes "then were burned by Kansas troops" in the escalating guerrilla war. As one historian has pointed out, "This was the most drastic measure taken against civilians during the Civil War prior to General Sherman's march to the sea." When Sherman marched across Georgia, he did nothing new or innovative; he simply used the Northern army to bring war home to civilians in a way that Southerners east of the Mississippi had never experienced on such a grand scale. Naturally, as the Savannah campaign unfolded, the city's residents hoped that Sherman would not come in their direction. When he did turn toward the port city, therefore, the actual event was psychologically devastating. Sherman understood perhaps better than most military men and politicians alike the importance of bringing the war to the home and hearth of the Southern family, and he intended to make the people in the Confederacy understand that overwhelming cultural chaos and personal ruin was going to be the result of their decision to tear the nation apart.[2]

I begin this story with Savannah, a city free from occupation as Christmas 1864 approached, and end with Savannah transformed, a conquered city where the inhabitants tried to celebrate the holiday season with enemy troops in the streets. In addition, Sherman had left frightened, disheartened, and hungry people all the way back to Atlanta. Nevertheless, he did not authorize a scorched-earth policy, even though many families had to struggle to find food in the wake of his armies, and recovery was difficult and slow. There was pillaging, to be sure, yet Sherman's soldiers did not murder civilians, nor did they destroy all the towns in their path on a scale seen in both earlier and later wars in world history.

Americans, however, do not live in a world measured against European or world history. Although the march to the sea pales in comparison to events worldwide, for the people of Georgia it was a vicious episode unparalleled in their immediate past. To them, it was unrestricted war on a scale unmatched by any of their own life experiences. Sherman himself, though, felt that he had "done nothing wonderful or new." He had only wanted the enemy to feel the "effects of war [and to see] how the Power of the United States can reach him in his innermost recesses." This goal he accomplished.[3]

Although Sherman carried out his mission, the march to the sea was not total war as twentieth-century historians came to define that term; it did not even come close to the ruthless warfare that Sherman later waged against American Indians in the West. It was certainly war on a grand scale, and Sherman told his wife that all "retire before us, and desolation is behind. To realize what war is one should follow our tracks."[4] What Sherman accomplished between Atlanta and Savannah was to bring the war home to civilians in a way they could not have imagined; he knew that to have its fullest impact, war had to be experienced firsthand. Nonetheless, the limits to warfare as he waged it were clearly beyond the bounds of what his enemies expected of a civilized nation, thus increasing the devastating emotional effect of his actions.

There is an unmistakable irony here. Only a few years before, both Northerners and Southerners had called themselves Americans. When the war came, both sides claimed to be the inheritors of the legacy of 1776. Sherman's march from Atlanta to Savannah was an event unprecedented in American history: American soldiers operating against American civilians in order to end the war so that all could be called Americans again. Sherman understood that to accomplish that end, he dared not entirely lay waste the land and its people. His march across Georgia had to be restricted if reunion was the ultimate goal. It was mainly his rhetoric that approached total war, for he used words in place of deeds. "Until we can repopulate Georgia, it is useless to occupy it," he wrote, "but the utter destruction of its roads, houses, and people will cripple their military resources. . . . I can make this march, and make Georgia howl." The impact of such words was lasting. Two years earlier, in October 1862, he had written of the people of Mississippi, "They cannot be made to love us, but may be made to fear us, and dread the passage of troops through their country." He rarely carried out his threats against the South in full, but his words would resonate through the generations, and his march to the sea would become synonymous with warfare against civilians despite its relative moderation. Retribution was saved for South Carolina, the state he blamed for bringing the nation to war.[5]

This work follows Sherman's trail from Atlanta to Savannah and shows that his war of words was far more devastating to the Southern nation than the actual events along his route. The march across Georgia was his idea alone, and it would be Sherman who changed forever the way Americans viewed warfare. His Savannah campaign in the fall of 1864 and his march through South Carolina early in 1865 only fulfilled what he had prophesied earlier, in 1862: "We cannot change the hearts of those people of the South, but we can make war so terrible that they will realize the fact that however brave and gallant and devoted to their country, still they are mortal and should exhaust all peaceful remedies before they fly to war."[6]

NOTES

1. *The Letters of William Gilmore Simms*, 5 vols., ed. Mary C. Simms Oliphant, Alfred Taylor Odell, and T. C. Duncan Eaves (Columbia: University of South Carolina Press, 1955), 4:471.

2. Michael Fellman, *Inside War: The Guerrilla Conflict in Missouri During the American Civil War* (New York: Oxford University Press, 1989), 95. The fighting in Kansas and Missouri often involved irregular troops while Sherman brought war home to civilians with soldiers in the U.S. Army.

3. *Sherman's Civil War: Selected Correspondence of William T. Sherman*, ed. Brooks D. Simpson and Jean V. Berlin (Chapel Hill: University of North Carolina Press, 1999), 810–11.

4. Ibid., 657. Although Sherman made this comment in reference to his campaign from Chattanooga to Atlanta, it was his intention to continue his war against civilians until the conflict ended.

5. William T. Sherman, *Memoirs of General William T. Sherman*, 2 vols. (1875; reprint, New York: Da Capo Press, 1984), 2:111, 118, 126–27; U.S. War Department, *The War of the Rebellion: A Compilation of the Official Records of the Union and Confederate Armies*, 128 vols. (Washington, DC: Government Printing Office, 1880–1901), 39, pt. 3, 162; 30, pt. 3, 698; 17, pt. 2, 261. All references to the *Official Records* (hereafter cited as *O.R.*) are to series 1 unless stated otherwise.

6. The march through South Carolina was far more devastating than the campaign across Georgia. *O.R.* 17, pt. 2, 261.

LIST OF MAPS

CHAPTER ONE

"A HAVEN OF BLISS"
Savannah

SAVANNAH, ALIVE WITH FOLIAGE, was an enormous garden in the spring and summer. Flowers and blooming shrubs surrounded many of the larger dwellings, and open expanses gave rise to lush grass, bushes, and trees. Broad thoroughfares intersected squares planted with oaks and evergreens, and the wide avenues reflected the spacious feeling suggested in the name Savannah. Rows of residences built flush with the street had gardens in the rear enclosed by brick walls, allowing the city's wealthiest residents to enjoy their privacy. Recessed doorways, delicate iron handrails, and dormer windows distinguished the elegant homes near the river. Throughout the city ornate churches vied in beauty with the fashionable dwellings. To one visitor, Savannah resembled a quiet English village where nothing ever changed, and a Northern-born soldier wrote in 1849 that "beautiful crepe myrtle bloomed in the yards of the wealthy while the lilac shed its fragrance around the abodes of the lowly. Roses, blooming and fresh, bordered the walks about the lawns, and from the wisteria twining itself over verandas hung clusters of flowers in reckless profusion."[1]

In the years before the war, Savannah natives had welcomed soldiers of the U.S. Army. One of them, John C. Tidball, a young Ohioan fresh out of West Point, observed that Savannah "had the reputation, and very justly, of being one of the most desirable posts in the army. In general tone, and genuine hospitality and refinement its society was of the best in the land, and welcomed officers of the army to it without question." Enthralled by the city, soldiers often married local women. As a result, observed Tidball, many families were "connected with the military service." Not only did this young man recognize the familial connection between the army and the city, he also noted that he had arrived in the "springtime of loveliness" and "landed in a haven of bliss."[2]

A traveler arriving in Savannah by boat, however, saw a bustling commercial port rather than a genteel Southern city. Though

1

located in coastal Chatham County, Savannah does not lie directly
on the Atlantic coast but is situated approximately eighteen miles
up the Savannah River. River Street, often crowded with jostling
humanity, snakes along the base of a high bluff built from the bal-
last stones of earlier vessels. Bay Street, usually called "the Bay,"
parallels River Street but at the top of the bluff. A lighthouse, erected
in the late 1850s and known as the Beacon Light, was described as
"altogether a beautiful and graceful structure" that "served as an
ornament for that part of the Bay." Its gaslight burned twenty-four
hours a day after city fathers realized they could save money by
keeping it lighted all the time rather than paying a keeper to at-
tend to it daily. According to one description, it was "a dark bronze
green, and fitted with a sixth order" Fresnel lens that emitted a red
light. This unique structure guided ships up the river and over the
wrecks (some dating to the American Revolution) to the safety of
the pier.[3]

Savannah waterfront, view one. Photo by George Barnard, 1866 (National Archives)

Before the war, wagons filled with cotton and tobacco from South
Carolina and inland Georgia filled the open area between Bay Street
and the numerous buildings housing the cotton traders. Factors
Row, which took its name from the factors or agents who ran the
prosperous cotton trading businesses, consisted of buildings, some
four stories high, between Bay Street and the busy docks along River
Street. Many businesses proclaimed in bold letters New York as
the site of their headquarters, and Savannah had become one of
the foremost commercial exchanges in the South; three railroads,
carrying cotton and timber to vessels headed north, terminated in
the city. In 1860 some 547,037 bales of cotton had left the docks in
the steady procession of ships down the river, and Savannah's ex-

ports totaled nearly $19 million. (Eli Whitney, who had worked as a tutor at Mulberry Grove, near Savannah, had invented the cotton gin there in the 1790s.) In return, foreign vessels brought English wool and cotton cloth, French wine, Cuban and Virginian tobacco, and coveted silk and lace. In the busy summer months many foreign ships lay at anchor, discharging their cargo and taking on local produce. The days were feverishly busy, but foreigners found life pleasant. The town was splendidly supplied with fresh meat and fish, including such delicacies as shrimp and oysters.

Savannah waterfront, view two. Photo by George Barnard, 1866 (National Archives)

Along the piers the tide rose and fell twice a day, and the smell of salt sea air testified to the nearness of the ocean, which also attracted visitors once the hot, humid summers, with their dangerous tropical diseases, ended. The scent of rope and tar permeated the wharves and warehouses as merchants, sea captains, and sailors from many lands looked for diversions in a variety of places, including the bawdy houses along the river where a woman's company could be enjoyed for a small sum. But most visitors did not see the port; instead, they stayed at one of the fashionable hotels where servants met their every need with alacrity.

Even after war came in 1861, ships still docked at the port. The U.S. Navy barred entrance to the river in 1862, but skilled blockade runners arrived regularly to delight patrons who prized items from abroad. Even as late as November 1864, a Confederate soldier wrote home that some men were "going to Europe with 8000 bales of Cotton to buy machinery for [the] Govt." One imported shipment in 1864 offered twenty chests of black tea, ten sacks of crushed sugar, ten sacks of fine coffee, and other items such as twine for cotton bags and Castile soap. All of this was sold at auction. The continued arrival of imported Bourbon whiskey and pure port wine indicated that Savannah's gentry had no intention of letting the war interfere with their comforts, even though it had diminished the city's commercial importance. Tradespeople, artisans, and idlers could be seen on Bay and River Streets, along with numerous soldiers in Confederate gray. Carts and wagons struggled through this flow of people around the wharves. At the taverns, women of the evening continued to ply their trade, unaffected by the nation's escalating conflict.[4]

Local residents also clustered in the city market, where people took their baskets to shop for all kind of delicacies. A fire in 1820 had destroyed the old buildings, and a debate had erupted over whether to move the marketplace farther from the docks. The suggestion fell on deaf ears, and the enterprise reopened in its old location with beef, veal, mutton, pork, fish, fresh fruit, and vegetables displayed by merchants. A shopper could find women of color shelling beans in big flat baskets or selling treats; among the most popular was a thin wafer cooked on the spot in long-handled wafer irons. Other open-air stalls offered baskets, flowers, and houseplants; potted palmettos were particularly popular inland. The resourceful shopper could purchase oysters and shrimp in spite of the Union blockade. And above the din of bartering, chickens, ducks, and turkeys squawked as the slaves picked out the best for their owners' evening meal.

Unfortunately, prices reflected conditions in the Confederacy, and the cost of goods rose as the value of Confederate money dropped. By August 1864 a 6-month subscription to the *Savannah Republican* set the reader back $20, a significant increase over the rate in the war's first year. One man even claimed to have paid $35 a pound for coffee, although a woman noted several weeks later that a pound of coffee cost her only $7.00. Throughout the South, merchants often scorned Confederate money and preferred to barter. But in Savannah there were actually few severe shortages; the city was too far removed from the devastation caused by the armies. Confederate money therefore remained the accepted means of payment. Basic goods were not hard to obtain, and the people wanted for little. Women might not wear the latest fashion, but residents were much better off than Confederates in other parts of the South where shortages made life harsh.[5]

Away from the noisy piers and markets, an Old World charm was reflected in Savannah's architecture. Its founder, James Oglethorpe, had planned the city's streets around squares, and the finer houses, set in the subtropical greenery, presented a calm beauty unknown in Georgia's inland cities. As in other cosmopolitan areas, though, fires were a constant threat, and after the first major fire in the mid-1700s, the city fathers passed a law prohibiting the repair or new construction of wooden chimneys. Brick became the building material of choice, and with this change came more permanent structures with larger rooms, loftier ceilings, and decorative details. The arrival from England of young William Jay marked a milestone in the city's architectural standard. Jay's restrained Regency creations combined perfect proportions with delicate classical details.

Despite the growing number of residences built during the early 1800s, the homes of many of the city's wealthier residents remained reminiscent of Europe, and the architecture reflected a marked English influence. Although some of the foundations were tabby, a mixture made locally of lime and oyster shells, most houses were constructed of brick and stucco. "Savannah Gray" brick, known for its distinctive color, was fired at the kiln on Henry McAlpin's plantation outside of town, and in 1835 the McAlpin House was built of easily repaired stuccoed-over brick, a wise choice in an area subject to occasional earthquakes or hurricanes.

Many visitors found the most striking feature to be Forsyth Park, authorized in 1851 by an act of the city council and named for Georgia's former governor, John Forsyth. The park's 20 acres covered seven blocks. A tree-lined green boasted magnolias, camphor, mimosa, and dense rows of flowering bushes. Springtime produced a sea of blooming azaleas, wisteria, and dogwood. A graceful fountain with elegant statues dominated the landscape. Savannah's militiamen had paraded across the grounds before heading off to war, and even when the commons no longer hosted militia drills, Sunday afternoon remained a popular time to stroll along the paths and enjoy the peaceful beauty.

Beyond the urban area, rice fields stretched for acres along the marshy shores of tidal water courses, and sea island cotton, a particular coastal strain, covered seemingly endless tracts. Moreover, visitors to the planters' homes often "went away praising the abundant variety of savory food that loaded the table: cured meats, preserves, fresh vegetables and brandy, all products of the plantation." A traveler in the 1850s had observed that upon his approach to his host's dwelling he had passed through "the proverbial avenue of live oaks draped with moss and found the household economy carried on in a style appropriate to a wealthy and cultured gentleman's home." The semitropical landscape alternated between swampland and hammocks where majestic live oaks and tall pine trees intermingled with a dense undergrowth of cedars and palmettos. Occasionally, the traveler caught a glimpse of a farmer's shack amid cypress swamps where alligators and snakes lurked in the shadows.[6]

Like all Southern cities, Savannah had a mixed population, comprising grandees and tradesmen, poor whites, slaves, and free people of color. The 1860 census count of 22,292 included 8,470 (38 percent) blacks. This one-third-plus of Savannah's population secretly supported a Union victory. Among the city's businessmen, commission merchants, and cotton agents were some of the state's wealthiest slaveowners. Yet visitors seldom commented on slavery or recorded impressions of the city's poverty. The tropical beauty of the city's squares often masked these unpleasant realities beyond the town's heart.

Much of the wealth of Savannah residents rested on plantations in the Low Country where the slave system was a pillar of the economy. One slave sale in 1859 had drawn national attention when *New York Tribune* editor Horace Greeley sent a reporter to cover the event. More than 430 slaves were transported three miles west of the city by rail, housed in racehorse stables, and sold at auction, netting the owner more than $300,000. For Northern readers avid to hear about the inhumanities of slavery, the reporter declared that the slaves "were examined with as little consideration as if they had been brutes indeed; the buyers pulling their mouths open to see their teeth, pinching their limbs to find how muscular they were, walking them up and down to detect any signs of lameness, [and] making them stoop and bend in different ways that they might be certain there was no concealed rupture or wound." And the story of the *Wanderer*, a vessel that landed some 400 Africans along the lower Georgia coast that same year, was well known.

Moreover, reopening the African slave trade—illegal since the early 1800s—had become a controversial issue throughout the South.[7]

The election of Abraham Lincoln as president of the United States in 1860 forced Southerners to reassess their loyalty to the Union. Orators denounced the Republican Party and pointed out the threat it posed to Southern institutions. In November 1860 the people of Savannah raised a flag of Southern independence, and one banner pictured a coiled rattlesnake and the words "Our Motto Southern Rights, Equality of the States, Don't Tread on Me." After South Carolina seceded in December, the city's residents began wearing secession cockades made of palmetto leaves to show their support for the Palmetto State. Men met at the Masonic Hall and Firemen's Hall to protest the injustices of the U.S. government and voice their objections to the "black Republican" who had won the election.[8] Secessionists harangued the crowds, including one young law student who proclaimed, "Let us not be backward in this matter; we are now delaying too long, for I have just learned that the ordinance of secession, if not already adopted, will soon be passed by that gallant little state, Texas!" Howls of laughter swept through the spectators at the speaker's inaccurate description of the Lone Star State.[9]

The swelling patriotism infected almost everyone. Two incidents in South Carolina—the evacuation of Fort Moultrie and the Federals' occupation of Fort Sumter in Charleston harbor in late 1860—seemed too close for comfort. In January 1861, Governor Joseph E. Brown of Georgia issued orders for Colonel Alexander R. Lawton to take Fort Pulaski on Cockspur Island, a massive masonry fortification that stood at the entrance to the Savannah River. Colonel Charles H. Olmstead recalled, "Upon the issue of this order the city was in a fever of excitement. Here at last was the first step of actual war."[10]

Still, it was several months before the first indication that the nation was really at war reached Savannah. In the summer of 1861, Josiah Tattnall manned four tugs and a river steamer and began patrolling the coastline from South Carolina to Florida. This so-called Mosquito Fleet could do little when faced with the power of the U.S. Navy, however. In November, Union vessels appeared at the mouth of the river. After they bombarded Tybee Island, several hundred Union troops moved ashore, and Tattnall wisely steamed upriver to safer waters. By December, more than 1,000 enemy soldiers had landed and begun preparations for an assault on Fort Pulaski. Concern for the Georgia coast prompted the Confederate government in Richmond to send General Robert E. Lee south; he spent November to February 1862 strengthening the defenses and building more fortifications and batteries around Savannah. Lee knew the terrain, for as a young soldier just out of West Point he had been stationed at the Georgia port during the early days of Fort Pulaski's construction. Now, under his leadership, the garrisons at Pulaski and upstream at Fort Jackson, just outside Savannah, were reinforced.

Fort Pulaski (United States Army Military History Institute—hereafter USAMHI)

At the outset of the war, recalled Savannah's mayor, Charles C. Jones Jr., the attention of the military commanders "had been mainly directed to the construction of fortifications for the protection of the city against water attacks and expeditions advancing directly from the coast. The likelihood of any demonstration from the rear had . . . been deemed so remote, and the probability of an attack from the coast so imminent on more than one occasion, that most of the available labor had been expended in the erection and arming of batteries to control the water approaches to the city, and in the construction of substantial earth works covering the eastern and southern exposures of Savannah." The water batteries included Fort Bartow, located at Causton's Bluff near where St. Augustine Creek met the Savannah River. Several other fortifications protected the city, and earthworks outside Savannah, such as Fort McAllister on the Ogeechee River, were reinforced.[11]

In the war's first year, residents felt safe under the protection of Fort Pulaski. Behind its walls of masonry more than seven feet thick, almost 400 men manned its forty-eight guns. Yet in spite of all the preparations, Union forces demanded its surrender on April 10, 1862. The Rebels refused, of course, and when Union batteries on Tybee Island opened fire, no one in Savannah believed that Pulaski would fall since it was beyond the effective range of conventional artillery. But fire from newly introduced rifled cannon punched through the fort's walls and rattled windows in the city. When the defenders surrendered after thirty-six hours of bombardment, panic spread throughout south Georgia.

The surrender of Pulaski and the large numbers of Federal troops encamped only a few miles from Savannah alarmed coastal residents. Governor Brown rushed more troops to the coast and impressed slaves to construct additional fortifications. Even free blacks were forced to work on the defenses. But throughout 1863 and 1864, although the Union navy probed up and down the coast and even burned the town of Darien in June 1863, Savannah remained unharmed. Closing the port seemed to have satisfied Northern interests, and the Federal military made no other serious effort to capture Savannah. As a result, a strange sense of security led residents to believe themselves immune from invasion.[12]

To the south, Fort McAllister, sixteen miles outside of Savannah, was important to the city's defensive perimeter. A massive earthwork which guarded the city's "back door," it resisted several bombardments from the Union fleet, for the shells sank harmlessly into the fort's earthen walls. After an attack in early 1864 in which the fort's commander died, the job of defending Savannah fell to Captain George W. Anderson of the Republican Blues. The Confederates knew that if McAllister fell, the city would follow; as long as the fort held, Savannah was secure.

Still, although the city remained far from the front and residents had little fear for their own personal safety, the war touched them in numerous ways. Most Georgians who had enlisted in the Confederate army in 1861 had rushed off to Virginia to fight. By 1862, many of those men were coming home, either wounded or dead. The almost daily funerals steadily increased the number of graves around Savannah as the war wore on. Laurel Grove Cemetery, established at the southwestern edge of the city in the early 1850s, soon became the final resting place of many Confederates from coastal Georgia. Among them was Francis S. Bartow, a Savannah native who fell leading Georgians at First Manassas in July 1861. Varina Davis, wife of the Confederate president, had personally carried the news to Louisa Bartow, who had accompanied her husband to Virginia. "As soon as I saw Mrs. Davis's face," Mrs. Bartow recalled, "I knew it all. . . . I knew it before I wrapped the shawl about my head." Her husband, a popular local lawyer, had raised the Oglethorpe Light Infantry and filled it with the scions of Savannah's society. As chairman of the Confederate Committee of Military Affairs, he had also been responsible for the gray color of Rebel uniforms. At the beginning of the war, Bartow had declared, "Let it come now, I am ready for it. . . . I would peril all, ALL, before I will abandon our rights in the Union or submit to be governed by an unprincipled majority." He was the first man in the state to lead a volunteer militia company off to fight, and after he died, three Savannah aldermen traveled to Charleston to accompany his body home. Bartow lay in state at the city council chamber for several days, his coffin covered with a Confederate flag bearing "chaplets of laurel," and four gray horses pulled the hearse to Laurel Grove in the "most solemn and imposing spectacle we have ever witnessed."[13]

Bartow was the first prominent Georgian to die, but in that same battle six Sunday school chums from Savannah's Independent Presbyterian Church also fell. As the bodies were returned home in January 1862, escorting coffins from Charleston became a melancholy routine. Moreover, as the fighting progressed and the number of dead increased, Savannah families quickly learned the price of their decision to go to war. Residents came to expect deaths from the Virginia theater since thousands of Georgians served with General Lee. Besides Laurel Grove, many Confederates were also buried at Bonaventure, a cemetery beside the Wilmington River, just over three miles southeast of the city. Following the war's outbreak and for many years after the fighting ceased, gravestones commemorating the region's loss continued to appear there, each standing ghostly white against the backdrop of greenery and Spanish moss that draped the large oak trees in the historic old burial ground. In December 1864 a Union general who had entered Savannah with Sherman observed: "There was one place . . . of which the people seemed very proud. This was Bonaventure, the cemetery."[14]

The news from the fighting in Virginia certainly saddened friends and families, but the city's residents could still take comfort in the belief that their homes remained safe from invaders. Most people believed that the Union cry, "On to Richmond," would never be duplicated in southeast Georgia. Even as late as the summer of 1864, while William Tecumseh Sherman moved deeper into north Georgia, it was hard to imagine that a war was raging less than 300 miles away. As Union soldiers fought the Rebel defenders outside Atlanta in July, Savannah gentry could choose Shakespearean comedy or tragedy, since theaters were offering performances of both *The Taming of the Shrew* and *Hamlet*. For those who wanted something more contemporary, there was the "beautiful drama" titled *The Conscript*, costing the same $2.00 as in January, when Miss Ella Wren had appeared as Lucretia Borgia. In July 1864, theater tickets ranged from 75 cents for the "colored gallery" to $2.00, though a private box cost $10 to $12, depending on location.[15]

Bonaventure Cemetery (USAMHI)

In their efforts to maintain a sense of normality, a night at the theater often reminded the city's residents that Savannah lay out of harm's way. In any case, the people firmly believed that the city offered nothing that would draw the Union's attention. It was not a military stronghold, and its wartime industry was insignificant. As long as the Confederate Army of Tennessee held Sherman in north Georgia, Savannah seemed secure. Even if the Rebels failed to contain Sherman and the Federals headed for the coast, they were unlikely to target Savannah. Nonetheless, hoping to keep the invaders engaged elsewhere and assure a strong Rebel presence to the north, citizens stepped up their contributions to the fund for the sick and wounded in the Confederate army. Even the colored congregation at St. Stephen's Church tendered a substantial $25. Sherman might be bearing down on Atlanta, but the city's men of letters continued to live as normally as possible. The Georgia Historical Society, founded twenty-five years earlier, planned its regular meeting for August 8.[16]

Only Georgians who lived along the coast felt the ever present shadow of soldiers in Union blue. Mary Jones, whose plantation was southwest of the city in Liberty County, wrote in June 1864 that she had heard of a landing of enemy soldiers on Wilmington and Whitemarsh Islands. Nonetheless, occasional raids by the Federals did not prevent her from moving freely between her home and Augusta and Savannah. She was less concerned for her own safety than for the welfare of friends and relatives in Atlanta. "We are having most solemn and interesting prayer meetings every afternoon at five o'clock," she wrote of a visit to Savannah. "Churches are crowded" with people praying for the safety of their loved ones. "Will not our Almighty Father, our Judge and Deliverer, hear and answer our cries for mercy?" she asked.[17]

Still, Confederate troops stationed on the barrier islands worried more about illness than about a Federal attack. Before the war, owners regularly abandoned their coastal plantations during the summer for safer sites inland; few people wanted to spend the hot humid months in the Low Country. Willie Smith, a Georgian assigned to the coastal defenses, told his sister that there was a great deal of typhoid fever among the soldiers. The Isle of Hope did not "seem to be so healthy as it used to be," he wrote. "It is very much overgrown and the turning up of the ground to make batteries may have made it sickly." Indeed, the sandy lowland proved a breeding ground for disease: the wide salt marshes, broken only by sluggish streams and encircled by dense foliage, provided a fertile environment for mosquitoes in the heat of the summer. Chiggers, ticks, and biting black flies also made life miserable. Smith remarked that it had been "a sickly summer" and there was "a great deal more sickness in the Corps this summer than there was last summer." In October he complained, "As usual the newspapers will lie about a thing. A few days ago the [Savannah] *Republican* had that there was no yellow fever in Savh." Indeed, the paper had published on the fourteenth, "YELLOW FEVER—We hear there are many extravagant reports in the interior reactive to the prevalence of yellow fever in Savannah.—some of the accounts represent our city as in a deplorable condition," but the press debunked stories of the spread of yellow fever. Fortunately, unlike the case in other regions of the Confederacy, quinine was generally available to treat the ill. Smith found time to take a "pleasant" buggy ride with a female friend, and the two rode "nearly all over the Island and got some pretty wild flowers." Moreover, he noted that proper food helped and assured his family, "We get milk and okra every now and then and manage to feed pretty well."[18]

Like Confederate soldiers on the barrier islands, Savannah residents worried more about immediate problems such as yellow fever than they did about a Union attack. They had come to expect occasional enemy incursions along the coast, but did not believe that the authorities in Washington would expend any energy to capture the city. As a result, city fathers tried hard to maintain business as usual, and on October 17, 1864, voters elected Richard Arnold mayor for the fifth time. (Arnold's first term had been in the 1840s, his second had begun in 1851, a third in 1859, a fourth in 1863). He had a long record in public service, both as mayor and a number of terms as alderman, and felt ready to meet any challenge.

As Arnold took the oath of office, the war still seemed a long way off. Families mourned casualties in Lee's army in Virginia and Hood's army outside Atlanta, but few people believed that their homes were in any real peril. In parlors throughout the city, voices sang about the war, and newly arrived sheet music brought high prices. Two of the more expensive were the popular "When This Cruel War Is Over" and "Lorena," each selling for $1.50. With adaption for the guitar or pianoforte, "The Standard Bearer" sold for $2.00. For those listening to these haunting refrains, Atlanta's troubles seemed far removed. War talk in Savannah continued to revolve around the fighting in Virginia, where friends and relatives were manning the trenches outside Richmond. Even the local papers devoted more coverage to the Virginia battles, relegating the fighting in Georgia to a small column. Savannah residents remained convinced that their city held nothing that would attract interest in Washington.[19]

Confederate leaders in Richmond also believed that since the Union navy had closed the port to regular shipping, the Federal government would ignore the city itself. To Northerners and Southerners alike it seemed that the capture of the river port would offer no significant military or political rewards. Even with Fort Pulaski

Union band at Fort Pulaski (USAMHI)

in Union hands and Union soldiers making occasional forays inland to remind Georgians of their presence, the inhabitants of Savannah still had an almost childlike trust in the Confederacy's
power to protect them from harm. It is true that by 1864 life was
harder for people living in southeast Georgia; they could no longer
find many items that had been readily available in the war's early
years. Prices for food had risen substantially, leaving poor families
struggling to survive. In April a small group of destitute women
raided stores, taking bacon and other foodstuffs. Although the authorities eventually arrested three women, no one was prosecuted;
the thieves were soldiers' wives whose children needed food, and
public sympathy was in their favor. Public displays of the poverty
caused by the war were rare; however, the city's middle- and
upper-class inhabitants considered the shortages a patriotic sacrifice. Savannahians made do with what they had; they repaired
clothing they could not replace, and patches on dresses and trou-
sers became symbols of loyalty to the cause. Local residents were
proud to point out that they were still free, unlike Confederates in
occupied cities such as New Orleans, Nashville, and Chattanooga.
Even though war weariness was slowly eroding the Confederacy's
patriotic underpinning, no one in Savannah really believed that
Union troops would ever march through the streets of a city that

was not a major military objective. This naive approach to war
would soon be challenged.[20]

NOTES

1. Works Progress Administration, *Savannah* (Savannah: Review Printing Co., 1937), 7–9; John C. Tidball, "A Northern Army Officer in Antebellum Savannah: The 1849 Memoirs of Second Lieutenant John C. Tidball,"
ed. Eugene C. Tidball, *Georgia Historical Quarterly* 84 (Spring 2000): 117;
Richard H. Haunton, "Savannah in the 1850s" (Ph.D. diss., Emory University, 1968), 26.
2. Tidball, "A Northern Army Officer in Antebellum Savannah," 117–19.
3. Haunton, "Savannah in the 1850s," 184; William Harden, *A History
of Savannah and South Georgia*, 2 vols. (1913; reprint, Atlanta: Cherokee
Publishing Co., 1969), 1:425. Harden was born in Savannah in 1844.
4. William Smith to Mother, November 9, 1864, in Arthur N. Skinner
and James L. Skinner, eds., *The Death of a Confederate: Selections from the
Letters of the Archibald Smith Family of Roswell, Georgia, 1864–1956* (Athens:
University of Georgia Press, 1996), 148; *Savannah Republican*, September 21,
1864.
5. Whittington B. Johnson, *Black Savannah, 1788–1864* (Fayetteville:
University of Arkansas Press, 1996), 169; Dolly Lunt Burge, *The Diary of
Dolly Lunt Burge, 1848–1879* (Athens: University of Georgia Press, 1997),
157.
6. Works Progress Administration, *Savannah*, 45.
7. Malcolm Bell Jr., *Major Butler's Legacy: Five Generations of a
Slaveholding Family* (Athens: University of Georgia Press, 1987), 323–24,
329–30; Preston Russell and Barbara Hines, *Savannah: A History of Her People
since 1733* (Savannah: Frederic C. Beil, 1992), 100–101.
8. F. N. Boney, "Georgia," in Richard N. Current, ed., *Encyclopedia of
the Confederacy*, 4 vols. (New York: Simon & Schuster, 1993), 2:668.
9. Harden, *Savannah and South Georgia*, 1:433.
10. Ibid., 435, quoting Charles H. Olmstead.
11. Charles C. Jones Jr., *The Siege of Savannah in December, 1864* (Albany, NY: Joel Munsell, 1874), 96.
12. Johnson, *Black Savannah*, 158–59.
13. Russell and Hines, *Savannah*, 102–3, 114; Robert H. Kerlin, *Confederate Generals of Georgia and Their Burial Sites* (Fayetteville, GA: Americana
Historical Books, 1994), 13–15, 140–41; Charles C. Jones Jr., to Rev. and
Mrs. C. C. Jones, July 29, 1861, in Robert Manson Myers, ed., *The Children
of Pride: A True Story of Georgia and the Civil War* (New Haven: Yale University Press, 1972), 723–24; Richard Owen and James Owen, *Generals at Rest:
The Grave Sites of the 425 Official Confederate Generals* (Shippensburg, PA:
White Mane Publishing Co., 1997), 57.
14. *The Memoirs of Brigadier General William Passmore Carlin, U.S.A.*,
ed. Robert I. Girardi and Nathaniel Cheairs Hughes Jr. (Lincoln: University of Nebraska Press, 1999), 163; Kerlin, *Confederate Generals of Georgia*,
13–15; 140–41; Owen and Owen, *Generals at Rest*, 57.
15. *Savannah Republican*, January 30, July 3, 1864.

16. Ibid., May 27, August 8, 1864.

17. Mrs. Mary Jones to Mrs. Mary S. Mallard, June 7, 1864, in Myers, *Children of Pride*, 1179.

18. William Smith to Helen Smith, July 9, 1864; William Smith to Mother, July 16, 1864; William Smith to Lizzie Smith, August 25, 1864; William Smith to Mother, August 29, September 7, and October 18, 1864, in Skinner and Skinner, *Death of a Confederate*, 69–70, 76, 100–101, 105, 111, 133; *Savannah Republican*, October 14, 1864.

19. *Savannah Republican*, May 24, 1864.

20. Teresa Crisp Williams and David Williams, " 'The Women Rising': Cotton, Class, and Confederate Georgia's Rioting Women," *Georgia Historical Quarterly* 86 (Spring 2002): 76–77.

CHAPTER TWO

"THE BLUE JACKETS RULE THE DAY"
Atlanta

ATLANTA'S CROWDED STREETS, unlike Savannah's quiet squares, bustled with activity. As the leaves turned to orange in the autumn of 1864, men in Union blue strolled through the town and camped in its parks. Crudely built shanties cluttered the city's main square; wood for these huts came at the expense of nearby buildings. "It is strange to go about Atlanta now and see only Yankee uniforms," wrote a resident. "The City Hall is headquarters for the Provost Guard. The enemy behave themselves pretty well except in the scramble for liquor, during which every store in town nearly was broken into yesterday. . . . This afternoon three soldiers asked for dinner saying their rations had not come and they would pay for their dinner, so Sallie had some cooked for them." The Union military presence was everywhere.[1]

Men in uniform were nothing new to Atlanta residents, for the city's strategic railroad network had made it a military center during much of the war. Large numbers of Confederate troops had passed through on numerous occasions, and Union leaders had made it an objective when the spring campaign opened in 1864. During the fighting through the late spring and summer, the Confederates had fallen steadily back from the north Georgia mountains. Their retreat brought them to the city in August.

Then the Union siege began, with artillery pounding the city daily. Vacant structures bore the scars of shells, and empty field fortifications reminded remaining residents of the cost of secession. Abandoned houses lined the streets, and all that remained of the railroad depot was a charred remnant of the structure. That destruction, however, was not the result of the Union assault. As the Confederates evacuated the city, they had destroyed all the locomotives and ammunition cars, along with all military stores they could not take. On the night of September 1, Southern cavalrymen sparked fires, and the resulting explosions could be heard for miles. Violent tremors rocked houses near the site and terrified residents.

The following day, Mayor James M. Calhoun surrendered Atlanta, and the streets filled with men in blue. It took around twenty-four hours to establish a military government, and in that time the "boys had free access to the town and lett [sic] me tell you they made use of their liberty, every one was loadened down with plunder," noted one Union soldier. "About noon today the Yankees came in sure enough," observed resident Samuel Richards. "The Stars and Stripes were soon floating aloft over the city." Sherman set up headquarters in the home built originally by John Neal, whose son Andrew had lost his life in the trenches outside the city.[2]

One Union officer wrote his wife his impressions of "the great 'Golden Apple.'" Atlanta was, he decided, "more like a new, thriving Western city" than any other place he had visited in the South. Though most of the people had fled, the officer had heard rumors that the population had grown from its prewar count of around 10,000 to as much as 70,000 with the flood of refugees passing through ahead of Sherman's arrival. On high rolling land, Atlanta was subdivided by creeks forcing the streets to follow odd patterns, "breaking the continuity," and giving parts of the city a "very ragged appearance." Businesses, he judged, were of a "mediocre quality," and Atlanta had "none of that built-up, finished, moss grown, venerable, aristocratic air, so noticeable in Southern cities." Another soldier observed that in this city, covering a circle of about 4 miles, "no two houses hardly met, no street is graded or building lot leveled off." Unlike Savannah, Atlanta had not benefited from careful planning. Less than three decades old, the town had originally carried the name Terminus—because it marked the end of the Western & Atlantic Railroad, which ran northwest to Chattanooga, Tennessee—and was later called Marthasville; in the 1840s it became Atlanta, an appellation considered more suitable for an expanding commercial center. A young army officer known to his friends as "Cump" Sherman had visited the region on assignment with the army back in the days when there had been nothing more than a train depot and a few scattered houses.[3]

William Tecumseh Sherman was an enigmatic figure. His men knew that he had lived in the South before the Civil War and had many Southern friends. Officers and soldiers often found him an object of curiosity. Men who saw him for the first time commented on his appearance, for his deeply wrinkled countenance created the impression of a no-nonsense, hardened veteran. Yet to many soldiers he was simply "Uncle Billy." It was not uncommon for him to mingle with his troops and "talk good earnest common-sense with the person nearest him, regardless of rank." He always seemed to have "an oald stub of a sigar in his mouth," although one man recalled that he "never saw it lighted." Another soldier remarked: "He is a very nervous man and can't keep still a moment," and later told his mother, "The boys call him 'crazy Billy,' but there seems to be some 'method in his madness.' "[4]

Ulysses S. Grant's military secretary in the last year of the war, Adam Badeau, described Sherman as "tall, angular, and spare, as if his superabundant energy had consumed his flesh." He was "sandy haired, sharp featured; his nose prominent, his lips thin, his grey eyes flashing fire as fast as lightning on a summer's night." His "speech [was] quick, decided, [and] loud." High-strung and animated, he gestured wildly as his thoughts came "too fast for utterance." He was "nervously active in mind and body," Colonel Henry Stone added. "With a clear idea of what he wanted and an unyielding determination to have it, he made himself and everybody around him uncomfortable till his demands were gratified; and when that was done some other enterprise was undertaken, with the same tireless and exacting spirit."[5]

Sherman's popularity among the men rested on two recent developments: the victory at Atlanta and the way he had quickly worked to satisfy the wants of his soldiers as soon as the fighting ended. Before the Federals took the city, provisions had become scarce and expensive. Coffee sold for as much as $35.00, butter went for $20.00, and eggs topped out at $12.00 per dozen in Confederate money. After the army arrived, supplies of all kinds moved down the Western & Atlantic Railroad, for Northern engineers repaired rails almost as quickly as Southern cavalry destroyed them. The *Louisville Daily Journal* reported that "sutlers, artisans, and newsdealers" reached Atlanta daily, and stores quickly opened.[6]

Soldiers controlled access to and from the city and picketed the roads to prevent any surprise attack by the Confederate army. Although the Union men "generally behaved pretty well," observed one resident, they did tear down houses and fences to build shanties for housing. The town soon resembled a huge military camp, with temporary structures lining the main streets and covering the parks. "The Blue Jackets rule the day," a soldier wrote his mother. "The streets are crowded with them from morn to night, . . . truly it is a Yankee town now." Still, noted a Pennsylvania surgeon, the "men have behaved themselves the best I saw them either home or

William T. Sherman (National Archives)

abroad. Every man has seemed to be on his good behavior since we entered Atlanta."[7]

Union officers even organized concerts. One was held on September 24 at the Atheneum Theater on Alabama Street, after carpenters repaired holes in the roof left from the bombardment. The entertainment included a brass band, amateur vocalists, and a piano solo by a local woman. "We led a happy life in Atlanta," a soldier recalled. "On week nights the Opera House was run by a variety of troupes, the principal performers being furnished by the Third Wisc. Regt." On at least one occasion the standing-room audience included General Sherman.[8]

Although Sherman could occasionally enjoy evening entertainment, he spent most of the time contemplating his next campaign. With a Confederate army camped just a few miles away, he knew he had to make plans. Meanwhile, his army required food for the men and fodder for the thousands of horses and mules, and his supply line, running from Louisville through Nashville to Knoxville, was in constant danger of being disrupted by enemy horsemen.

During the fighting in the summer, Rebel troopers under Major General Joseph Wheeler had been a nuisance but had done little damage to the track. Yet Sherman recognized that if the Confederates decided to dispatch cavalry chief Nathan Bedford Forrest to eastern Tennessee, the situation would change. To prevent that possibility, he ordered his subordinates in western Tennessee to keep Forrest busy. In the meantime, Sherman told his wife, Ellen, that he had his men practicing the "art of foraging and they take to it like Ducks to water. They like pigs, sheep, chickens, calves and Sweet potatoes better than Rations."[9]

As scavenging through the country became essential for survival, one of Sherman's soldiers commented, "Just now foraging or raiding parties are all the rage with us, in fact it was a necessity for the mules were dying fast." He recounted the exploits of one party that scoured the countryside, consisting of three brigades, two batteries, and a battalion of cavalry with 500 wagons. "They went about 25 miles, were gone 4 days & brought back every wagon full of corn or sweet potatoes, as well as any number of sheep, calves, pigs, fowls, etc. The men lived high off the country and brought back lots of plunder." A Southerner who rode through the region northwest of Atlanta commented, a "more desolate country I never saw; not a domestic animal or fowl, and scarcely a bird could be seen. . . . The fences had all been torn down . . . and the people were subsisting on corn bread made of grated meal and syrup made in the crudest manner."[10]

During the summer campaigns, local residents had generally seen only cavalry. But in early November a Georgian in Powder Springs, a little town north of Atlanta near Marietta, wrote his

Joseph Wheeler (USAMHI)

sister that "the infantry came around, and I never saw meaner men before." Some killed the hogs, chickens, and a goat while others ransacked the house. "Carrie begged them not to take all she had. Their answer was that many a woman below was left without anything at all. 'Why,' said Carrie. 'What am I to do? How am I to live if you take all that I have?' 'Go North!' was the reply, as curtly as it could be spoken." Nevertheless, after killing all the animals, the soldiers gave the woman a piece of the hog and the head, and "altogether what she got back would nearly make a whole one." The soldiers, known to Confederates as the "Blue Devils," foraged liberally, often using the threat of violence as a means to intimidate civilians. Elizabeth Perkerson also wrote of a visit from the "Blue Devils," although she did admit that "a great many of them tried to be very friendly."[11]

Still, Sherman had no intention of wintering in Atlanta; he planned to link up with the U.S. Navy somewhere along the coast. His exact destination was another matter. The logical choice appeared to be Mobile. When Grant became general-in-chief in 1864, he still believed that the Alabama port should be a major objective and thought the army in Louisiana under Major General Nathaniel P. Banks should move in that direction. But operations begun by Grant's predecessor, Henry Halleck, were already under way: General Banks had orders to move up the Red River toward Shreveport and link with a Federal army coming from Little Rock. Grant later wrote that he had "strenuously" opposed the decision to march through Louisiana "but acquiesced because it was the order of my superior at the time." Sherman, in fact, had hoped to have command of the expedition. He had a personal interest, having once been the superintendent of the Seminary of Learning near Alexandria, a town along the proposed route. "I wanted to go up Red River," he had confided to Ellen, "but as Banks was to command it in person I thought [it] best not to go." Instead, Sherman had headed for Georgia, leaving behind 10,000 men to accompany Banks on the campaign in April.[12]

Grant later pointed out that he had "tried for more than two years to have an expedition sent against Mobile when its possession by us would have been of great advantage." Even as late as September 1864, many authorities in Washington still thought Mobile remained Sherman's goal; Halleck had already started forwarding supplies to Pensacola for Sherman's anticipated change of base. The former general-in-chief believed that Montgomery and Selma were more important than any other Southern cities Sherman might capture and that the Alabama River was the most navigable of any in the lower South. Halleck also thought that from a military standpoint, moving into Alabama would not leave Tennessee or Kentucky uncovered. Finally, marching through Alabama would bring a valuable region of the Confederacy under Union control.[13]

So why did Sherman not choose the Mobile route? On September 20 he told Grant that he proposed to cross Georgia instead. "Where a million of people live my army won't starve," he pointed out. Furthermore, he argued, Union "possession of the Savannah River" would be "fatal to the possibility of a Southern independence." Controlling the river meant controlling Georgia, and Sherman believed that the Confederacy could never overcome the loss of the Empire State of the South. On October 1 he specifically requested permission to "destroy Atlanta, and then march across Georgia to Savannah or Charleston, breaking roads and doing irreparable damage." This was clearly not what Halleck wanted. Once the spring campaign had opened, it was always assumed that after Sherman captured Atlanta he would link up with Major General Edward R. S. Canby, who commanded the Military Division of Western Mississippi, and take Mobile. But since Canby had provided troops for other campaigns, he could no longer offer adequate assistance to Sherman. Besides, Admiral David G. Farragut had closed Mobile Bay in early August, thus diminishing that port's importance. Moreover, Sherman assured Grant that his march across Georgia "could be made in the winter," an important consideration for a campaign planned late in the year.[14]

Whatever direction Sherman went, he knew he did not have the complete support of the administration. As a politician, Lincoln's primary concern was the upcoming presidential election, and he did not want anything to disrupt the recent gains that the military had made in the war of words played out in the press. Although Grant had not broken the stalemate in Virginia, Farragut had closed Mobile Bay; Sherman had captured Atlanta in early September; and Philip Sheridan had devastated the Shenandoah Valley later in the month. Republicans used these victories to counter Democratic charges that the war was a failure. Lincoln worried that a Rebel army could destroy Sherman deep in Confederate territory, and if that happened, it might jeopardize his chance for a second term in the White House. Therefore, the president told the secretary of war that he felt "much solicitude" regarding the proposed march and hoped it would "be maturely considered." Grant, however, came to see the logic behind Sherman's reasoning and persuaded the president to consider the idea.[15]

While politics played out in Washington, Sherman continued to plan for a march to the coast. He had operated independently in the West for so long that he was confident of eventual permission.

Needing to ready the army for the new campaign, he ordered most civilians removed from Atlanta. He did not want his men distracted, nor did he want to have to worry about protecting women and children, so he issued orders expelling both Union and Confederate civilians; he wanted the city to become "a pure Gibraltar." Both the Confederate general John Bell Hood and Atlanta's mayor, James Calhoun, protested, but Sherman brushed aside the objections. "War is cruelty," he responded, "and you can not refine it."[16]

Unconcerned with the criticisms of his actions, Sherman went about the business of reorganizing the army. He wanted "to make Atlanta a pure military garrison or depot, with no civil population to influence military measures." He pointed out that a civilian population absorbed "the attention of officers in listening to everlasting complaints and special grievances that are not military." He intended for his officers to concentrate on military matters and not have them distracted by civilian problems. Sherman believed that armies "were not designed to meet the humanities of the case" but intended to further the winning of the war. He had told the Atlanta mayor, "We are not only fighting hostile armies, but a hostile people, and must make old and young, rich and poor, feel the hard hand of war. . . . We cannot change the hearts of those people of the South, but we can make war so terrible . . . that generations would pass away before they would again appeal to it."[17]

The decision to expel nonessential noncombatants proved popular in Northern circles. Henry Halleck assured Sherman that it had the full support of the War Department, that he thought the laws and usages of war justified such actions, and that he believed it was Sherman's duty to his own army. "We have fed this class of people long enough," he blustered. "I have endeavored to impress these views upon our commanders for the last two years. You are almost the only one who has properly applied them." Closer to home, Ellen Sherman, too, applauded her husband's decision. She thought the "insolent women" in particular should be punished, for it was "preposterous to have our Government feeding so many of their people."[18]

This step was the first of many actions Sherman took that would later cause Southerners to vilify his name. The Georgia press throughout the state blasted him for turning out helpless women and children. Moreover, if Southerners could have read his correspondence with Grant, their concern would have increased dramatically. Sherman told his superior in early October, "Until we

can repopulate Georgia, it is useless to occupy it, but the utter destruction of its roads, houses, and people will cripple their military
resources. . . . I can make the march, and make Georgia howl."[19]

Sherman's order gave Atlanta residents five days to prepare
for the trip south, and there was a temporary truce with the Confederates. As the civilians left the city, a soldier wrote, "It was a
very pitable sight . . . to behold little children almost naked and
many women barefooted." With nowhere to go, the refugees turned
to Governor Brown for assistance, and he, using funds designated
for the army, authorized the building of temporary shelters and
the purchase of food.[20] A woman in Culloden, not far from Macon,
described "one of the greatest stampedes I ever saw in my life"
when scores of refugees passed her home. The roads were thronged
with hogs, sheep, and cattle, female slaves and their children, and
wagons filled with white exiles. Fear permeated the air when the
travelers heard that the Yankees were near, and it quickly turned
to panic as the swarm of refugees tried to reverse direction. Soon,
however, it was discovered to be a false alarm, and the tired and
hungry outcasts continued on their way south.[21]

Meanwhile, Sherman and Hood agreed to a trade of around
2,000 prisoners. The Confederates desperately needed their men
back in the ranks, but Sherman refused to discuss a wider exchange
(although it could have freed Union men held at Andersonville),
agreeing to accept only those Federal soldiers who had been recently captured and were ready for active campaigning. He rejected
many of the prisoners transported from Andersonville to Atlanta
for consideration. A New Yorker who had been at Andersonville
for over six months complained that Sherman "selected only his
own command for exchange, and sent all the rest back to captivity!
All hope of exchange was not abandoned, and amid hearty curses
on the government, and Sherman, [Benjamin] Butler, and others,
the camp was wild with excitement, anger, and gloom." It was no
secret that Sherman preferred soldiers from the western armies, as
was evident in the men he picked for exchange. Naturally, those
captives returning to Andersonville grumbled that although they
received enough to eat, they had not been issued clothing, "which
was the least thing Sherman could have done." As a result, the prisoners looked "like skeletons in rags," and one of them noted that
"this act of Sherman's will kill hundreds, as all hope of ever getting out of this is gone."[22]

One of the fortunate soldiers with Sherman in Atlanta noted that the "Confederates had brought up a lot of our prisoners who do not come under the terms of the exchange. They are a sorry looking lot," and some who discovered that Sherman intended to send them back "made a break for our lines." Neither Union or Confederate soldiers fired on the pathetic runaways, and a number escaped.[23]

Sherman knew exactly how people would regard his actions. He was proud of his Atlanta campaign and told a friend he thought it would "compare well with that of the European Models." Even though he confided to his brother-in-law that he was "almost tired of playing war," he reveled in his new renown. He also knew his decision to evacuate Atlanta would reap criticism. "These fellows have a way of leaving us to take care of their families," he complained of the Rebels, "but when I took Atlanta I ordered them all to quit and a big howl is raised against my Barbarity—Butler is the Beast, Sherman the Brute & Grant the Butcher."[24]

Northerners saw Sherman as a hero. The people of Lancaster, Ohio, raised $1,700 to buy the general a horse and equipment. Although Sherman felt flattered that his "old Townsmen" would do something so considerate, he told his brother-in-law that he preferred riding his own horse, an animal named "Dick" which had been presented to him in Louisville. Dick suited his "style of riding exactly," he added. Besides, he had six other mounts that he could ride for "knocking about among our Lines, trains of wagons & camps." He wanted the new mount kept at Lancaster, provided it could be maintained "in full vigor by constant practice." He preferred a new animal to be a "free, bold, walker, trotter and canter, especially the former. He should 'take' a leap anything in reason, such as a fence, gully, or log. Should be well bitted to the curb, and not afraid of anything." He confided to his brother-in-law he had ridden four such horses during the war—three were dead; one had been killed under him. Dick was the fourth, and he was not yet eager for a replacement.[25]

As the general's plan developed, one soldier told his wife that "preparations are being rapidly made for one of Sherman's peculiar movements, which will transfer this army far from the scene of its present operations." Yet the troops knew little of what was in the wind, and the man added, "The whole programme may be changed; the movement may not begin at all, but I think it will."

Clearly, something was happening at army headquarters, and it had the troops anxious to find out what. Soldiers speculated that the destination was probably somewhere along the coast, for the alternative of following the Confederate army, observed one major, was "like an elephant chasing a mouse. . . . I believe we *are* going to do *something*, but I hardly dare guess what, yet." But another complained, "I cannot see how Sherman can move forward from Atlanta for we are now on 3/4 rations and not a pound of anything will come down for a week yet."[26]

Still, the soldiers prepared to move. One recalled that he gathered his "writing materials," but "old letters were re-read and burned" and photographs inspected before being tucked away. The companies packed their papers in small boxes that they were "allowed to carry in the regimental wagon" along with "a couple of shovels, pickaxes, and axes" for use in entrenching. In their knapsacks the men included such luxuries as soap and tea. Many veterans regretted leaving their comfortable lodgings in Atlanta, however. One soldier looked at his "miniature home" with the "little cupboard made by our own hands, the table, stools, bunks, shelves, and fireplaces, evidences of industry which we hoped long to enjoy."[27]

For his new campaign Sherman reorganized his army. Since John Schofield had gone to Knoxville to keep an eye on Hood, Sherman replaced him with Jacob Cox. George H. Thomas, who has assumed command at Nashville and was also awaiting Hood, was replaced by Ohio native Major General David S. Stanley (who had turned down a Confederate commission in 1861). The Sixteenth Corps was broken up and scattered between the Fifteenth and Seventeenth Corps. Sherman ordered the Fourth Corps from the Department of the Cumberland and the Twenty-third Corps from the Department of the Ohio to join Thomas.

In another important change, Sherman sent his cavalry commander, Major General James H. Wilson, to Nashville to deal with the Confederates, retaining only a small force under Judson Kilpatrick. This New Jersey–born brigadier general could be insufferable, and many Northern soldiers, particularly among the infantry, did not like him. Sherman even admitted, "I know that Kilpatrick is a hell of a damned fool, but I want just that sort of man to command my cavalry in this expedition." Moreover, Kilpatrick knew the Rebel cavalry commander, Joseph Wheeler, for the two were the same age and had been classmates at West Point.[28] Kilpatrick was young for a brigadier, only twenty-eight, and his reputation for "notorious immoralities" had preceded him west. Nicknamed "Kill-Cavalry," he seemed quite confident in his own abilities, and a major sarcastically told his wife that Kilpatrick was the "most vain, conceited, egotistical little popinjay I ever saw" with only one redeeming quality: he did not often drink to excess. He was, however, "a very ungraceful rider," pronounced the major, "looking more like a monkey than a man on horseback."[29]

Joe Wheeler, Kilpatrick's Georgia-born Confederate counterpart, also had an impressive record for such a young man. He had risen through the ranks all the way to major general. A conflict with Nathan Bedford Forrest had meant he was assigned to East Tennessee, far from Forrest's domain in the western part of the state. As a result, Wheeler headed the cavalry in the Army of Tennessee. Thus, as Sherman planned for the coming campaign, he knew his cavalry commander would face the young Confederate.

Sherman with his commanders (National Archives)

Sherman retained four veteran corps, dividing them into two wings. The men selected as wing commanders were both veterans with respected reputations, Oliver O. Howard and Henry W. Slocum. Howard, a native of Maine and a career military man, had graduated from West Point in 1854 an impressive fourth in a class of forty-six. He had fought in Virginia early in the war, losing his right arm at Fair Oaks in the spring of 1862. The loss did not slow him down, for he took part in the battles of Antietam, Fredericksburg, Chancellorsville, and Gettysburg before transferring to the Army of the Cumberland. He led a corps in the Chattanooga and Atlanta campaigns under Joseph Hooker, and he eventually succeeded to command of the Army of the Tennessee.

The New York–born Slocum had graduated from West Point two years earlier with an equally impressive ranking, seventh of forty-three. He had then left the army but reenlisted when the war began. He fought in Virginia and accompanied Howard to Tennessee in 1863. Slocum, however, refused to serve under Hooker, whom he disliked intensely, and threatened to resign. To defuse the situation, Slocum was assigned to Vicksburg; he did not join Sherman's army until Hooker had left. (Hooker resigned because he thought himself, rather than Howard, rightly entitled to command the Army of the Tennessee after James B. McPherson had been killed in July.)[30]

The right wing, under Howard, was composed of the Fifteenth and Seventeenth Corps. The Fifteenth, under Major General Peter J. Osterhaus, numbered 724 officers and 14,568 men and included divisions commanded by Brigadier Generals Charles R. Woods, William B. Hazen, John E. Smith, and John M. Corse. The Seventeenth was the smallest corps, with only 420 officers and 10,667 men. Under the overall command of Major General Frank P. Blair Jr., its divisions were led by Major General Joseph A. Mower and Brigadier Generals Mortimer D. Leggett and Giles A. Smith.[31]

Slocum's left wing comprised the Fourteenth and Twentieth Corps. The Fourteenth, with 556 officers and 12,397 men, was under Brevet Major General Jefferson C. Davis, with divisions commanded by Brigadier Generals William P. Carlin, James D. Morgan, and Absalom Baird. Finally, the Twentieth Corps had 602 officers and 12,862 men under Brigadier General Alpheus S. Williams, with divisions headed by Brigadier Generals Nathaniel J. Jackson, John W. Geary, and William T. Ward. Command of the cavalry, some 244 officers and 4,672 troopers, fell to Judson Kilpatrick. The effective strength of the army as reported on November 10 did not include the various artillerymen and a handful of cavalry attached to the Seventeenth Corps, which numbered an additional 1,833. The grand total was 59,545. The number would increase slightly before Sherman departed, for on November 30, returns showed 62,204 men.[32]

More than 60,000 soldiers constituted a large force, but the civilian workers, numerous wagons, draft animals, cavalry horses, and the cattle herded along for food increased the size dramatically. Sherman had done all he could to decrease the bulk, for he knew that unwieldiness would hamper his mobility. He had ordered surplus supplies and cumbersome artillery returned to Tennessee and had instructed the men to reduce their belongings to the bare necessities. He studied maps of middle Georgia carefully and calculated how far he could go before food and fodder became concerns. Since the march coincided with the fall harvest, moving through the rich agricultural regions would not be a problem, but he recognized that shortages could emerge as he neared the coast, and that knowledge increased his determination to link with the navy at the earliest opportunity.

While Sherman worked on strategy, he waited patiently for two events. The first he could predict accurately: the presidential election the second Tuesday in November. Although Lincoln had given a reluctant blessing to the march, he did not want Sherman to leave until after he was safely in the White House for another term. The delay annoyed Sherman, but he understood that he must honor the request. The second hurdle was not so easily projected. The general hoped the fall rains would pass before he left; he did not want his army mired in the red Georgia clay. He would later credit his success to a "Singular Capacity for knowledge of *Roads*, the resources of a Country, and the Capacity of my Command."[33]

When the two events occurred almost simultaneously, Sherman felt confident his luck would hold. On Tuesday, November 8, Lincoln won reelection by an electoral vote of 212 to 21. On that same day, as raindrops began to fall, Sherman telegraphed his commanders, "This is the rain I have been waiting for, and as soon as it is over we will be off." Henry Hitchcock entered in his diary, "We hope this means just what the General has been desiring,—that the fall rains should come all together, early in November, and give us fine weather for some weeks, which is what we want *now*."[34]

Sherman's goal was to break the South's will to fight, not to devastate the land and murder the people. He had enthusiastically told Grant in September that Southerners "may stand the fall of Richmond, but not all of Georgia. . . . If you can whip Lee and I can march to the Atlantic I think Uncle Abe will give us a twenty days' leave of absence to see the young folks." Winning the war, whatever it took, was certainly his intent. Yet the only incident of deliberate total destruction actually happened before Sherman left on his march when Cassville, a little town outside of Atlanta, was destroyed for providing a haven for Rebel cavalry. In early November, the commander of the Fifth Ohio Cavalry received orders to burn the village to the ground, a job the men accomplished with apparent relish.[35]

On the march to the sea, Sherman forbade soldiers to enter private homes, and corps commanders were to destroy houses, mills, barns, cotton gins, and other property only if their owners harbored Rebels attacking the Union columns or if the residents themselves had thwarted the Union advance. The officers could not stop all vandalism, however, and the men often simply ignored Sherman's directives. A Wisconsin soldier had confided to his fiancée in May 1864 that after twenty-three Rebels had surrendered, the Union soldiers had killed all of them. "When there is no officer with us, we take no prisoners," he confessed. Such acts, when an officer was not present, probably also took place on the march to Savannah.[36]

Sherman did authorize his army "to forage liberally on the country," insisting that the wagon trains keep at least "ten days' provisions for his command, and three days' forage." His instructions read: "Soldiers must not enter the dwellings of the inhabitants, or commit any trespass; but, during a halt or camp, they may be permitted to gather turnips, potatoes, and other vegetables, and to drive in stock in sight of their camp." Only regular foraging parties could gather provisions or travel any distance from the main columns. "In districts and neighborhoods where the army is unmolested, no destruction of such property should be permitted; but should guerrillas or bushwhackers molest our march, or should the inhabitants burn bridges, obstruct roads, or otherwise manifest local hostility," then army commanders should "order and enforce a devastation more or less relentless according to the measure of such hostility."[37]

The cavalry and artillery had authority to "appropriate freely and without limit" any horses, mules, or wagons. Sherman did add that soldiers should discriminate "between the rich, who are usually hostile, and the poor and industrious, usually neutral or friendly." The men were to "refrain from abusive or threatening language" and must "endeavor to leave with each family a reasonable portion for their maintenance." As for encouraging slaves who wanted to follow the army, Sherman reminded his commanders that they should keep in mind the "question of supplies" and that it was their "first duty" to "see to those who bear arms." Clearly, escaped slaves added an often unwanted burden on the quarter-masters.[38]

Sherman knew that wanton acts of destruction would do more to terrify civilians than anything his army could do in battle. He wanted to go after the heart and soul of the Southern nation and break the will of Confederates. He recognized the impossibility of policing 60,000 men, but he also understood that if he overlooked some unauthorized activities, those unsanctioned deeds would frighten the civilians more than an orderly advance. He later admitted to Halleck that some of his men were a "little loose in foraging, they 'did some things they ought not to have done,' yet, on the whole, they have supplied the wants of the army with as little violence as could be expected, and as little loss as I calculated." Sherman certainly understood that by turning a blind eye he had given tacit approval, while at the same time protecting his own reputation: after the march ended, he could remind critics that he had expressly disapproved any unauthorized acts of destruction.[39]

Even in his memoirs he expressed his awareness of the criticisms. He recounted that he had seen a soldier walk by with a "ham on his musket, a jug of sorghum-molasses under his arm, and a big piece of honey in his hand, from which he was eating." Seeing the general watching him, the man had remarked, "Forage liberally on the country," quoting from what he knew to be Sherman's orders. "On this occasion, as on many others that fell under my personal observation," later wrote Sherman, "I reproved the man, explained that foraging must be limited to the regular parties properly detailed, and that all provisions thus obtained must be delivered to the regular commissaries, to be fairly distributed to the men who kept their ranks."[40]

Sherman also knew that his campaigns would become part of American history. "I do honestly believe I crave Peace as much as any man living," he wrote his wife's brother Phil, "and that in feeling and prejudice I have if anything leaned to the South, still in adherence to Principle I have steered my Course as straight as the currents of events would permit. If [in] spite of my efforts at mediocrity, and subordination, if my name must go to History, I prefer it should not as the enemy to the South." Uncertain about what the future held, he sent Ellen a short message on November 12: "We start today. . . . Write no more till you hear of me. Good bye. W. T. Sherman."[41]

NOTES

1. Samuel P. Richard Diary, entry dated September 4, 1864, quoted in Franklin M. Garrett, *Atlanta and Environs: A Chronicle of Its People and Events*, 3 vols. (New York: Lewis Historical Publishing Co., 1954), 1:637.

2. Letter dated September 4, 1864, quoted in Lee Kennett, *Marching through Georgia: The Story of Soldiers and Civilians during Sherman's Campaign* (1995; reprint, New York: Harper Perennial, 1996), 203; Richard Diary, entry dated September 2, 1864, quoted in Garrett, *Atlanta*, 1:636–37.

3. James A. Connolly, *Three Years in the Army of the Cumberland: The Letters and Diary of Major James A. Connolly*, ed. Paul M. Angle (Bloomington: Indiana University Press, 1959), 259; A. A. Hoehling, *Last Train from Atlanta: The Heroic Story of an American City under Siege* (New York: Thomas Yoseloff, 1958), 458.

4. Joseph T. Glatthaar, *The March to the Sea and Beyond: Sherman's Troops in the Savannah and Carolinas Campaign* (New York: New York University Press, 1985), 16; Charles W. Wills, *Army Life of an Illinois Soldier* (1906; reprint, Carbondale: Southern Illinois University Press, 1996), 314; *Soldiering with Sherman: Civil War Letters of George F. Cram*, ed. Jennifer Cain Bohrnstedt (DeKalb: Northern Illinois University Press, 2000), 142, 154.

5. Quoted in Alfred H. Burne, *Lee, Grant, and Sherman: A Study in Leadership in the 1864–65 Campaign* (1938; reprint, Lawrence: University Press of Kansas, 2000), 70–71.

6. Kennett, *Marching through Georgia*, 213.

7. Garrett, *Atlanta*, 1:643; soldier quoted in Kennett, *Marching through Georgia*, 206–7.

8. Kennett, *Marching through Georgia*, 214.

9. Sherman, *Sherman's Civil War*, 738–39.

10. Although this raid occurred in October, it was typical of most of the foraging around Atlanta. Garrett, *Atlanta*, 1:647. The Southerner is quoted in Kennett, *Marching through Georgia*, 237.

11. Mills Lane, ed., *"Dear Mother: Don't grieve about me. If I get killed, I'll only be dead": Letters from Georgia Soldiers in the Civil War* (Savannah, GA: Beehive Press, 1977), 333; idem., ed., *Times That Prove People's Principles: Civil War in Georgia: A Documentary History* (Savannah: Beehive Press, 1993), 206.

12. U. S. Grant, *Personal Memoirs of U. S. Grant*, 2 vols. (1885; reprint, Lincoln: University of Nebraska Press, 1996), 2:418; Sherman, *Sherman's Civil War*, 607.

13. Grant, *Personal Memoirs*, 2:647; *O.R.* 39, pt. 3, 25–26.

14. *O.R.* 39, pt. 2, 412; 39, pt. 3, 3.

15. *O.R.* 39, pt. 3, 222.

16. Stanley F. Horn, *The Army of Tennessee: A Military History* (Indianapolis: Bobbs-Merrill, 1941), 369.

17. Sherman, *Memoirs*, 2:111, 118, 126–27; *O.R.* 38, pt. 5, 1023; James M. McPherson, *Battle Cry of Freedom: The Civil War Era* (New York: Oxford University Press, 1988), 809.

18. *O.R.* 39, pt. 2, 503; John F. Marszalek, *Sherman: A Soldier's Passion for Order* (New York: Free Press, 1993), 286.

19. *O.R.* 39, pt. 3, 162.

20. Kennett, *Marching through Georgia*, 238.

21. Carrie V. Timberlake to Thomas W. Bartlett, December 1, 1864, Blanton Family Papers, Virginia Historical Society, Richmond.

22. Robert Knox Sneden, *The Eye of the Storm: A Civil War Odyssey*, ed. Charles F. Bryan Jr., and Nelson D. Lankford (New York: Free Press, 2000), 255. Sneden, a private and a mapmaker in the Fortieth New York Infantry, had arrived at Andersonville the last week of February. He wrote this entry on September 13. The men in prison partly blamed their incarceration on Butler, since it was widely believed that he opposed prisoner exchange unless black soldiers were also included—something the Confederacy resisted.

23. Theodore F. Upson, *With Sherman to the Sea: The Civil War Letters, Diaries, and Reminiscences of Theodore F. Upson*, ed. Oscar Osburn Winther (Baton Rouge: Louisiana State University Press, 1943), 127–28.

24. Sherman was referring to Benjamin Butler in New Orleans and Grant in the Virginia campaign of 1864. Sherman, *Sherman's Civil War*, 713, 715.

25. Ibid., 725.

26. Connolly, *Three Years*, 285–86; Cram, *Soldiering with Sherman*, 144.

27. Cram, *Soldiering with Sherman*, 149.

28. Ezra J. Warner, *Generals in Blue: Lives of the Union Commanders* (Baton Rouge: Louisiana State University Press, 1964), 267.

29. Connolly, *Three Years*, 348.

30. John Logan had initially been given command of the Army of the Tennessee but was relieved by Lincoln within a few days. Hooker was then serving as commander of the Twentieth Corps in the Army of the Cumberland, under the command of Thomas. Howard's accession to command of the Army of the Tennessee would not have placed Hooker under his command.

31. *O.R.* 44, 15–16.

32. Ibid.

33. Sherman, *Sherman's Civil War*, 786.

34. *O.R.* 39, pt. 3, 700; Henry Hitchcock, *Marching with Sherman: Passages from the Letters and Campaign Diaries of Henry Hitchcock*, ed. M. A. DeWolfe Howe (New Haven: Yale University Press, 1927), 42.

35. *O.R.* 39, pt. 2, 412–13. There were other small towns in Georgia—Griswoldville, Hillsboro, and Irwinton, for example—that suffered significant destruction.

36. *O.R.* 39, pt. 3, 713; James M. McPherson, *For Cause and Comrades: Why Men Fought in the Civil War* (New York: Oxford University Press, 1997), 154.

37. Sherman, *Memoirs*, 2:175.

38. Ibid., 175–76.

39. *O.R.* 44, 14.

40. Sherman, *Memoirs*, 2:181.

41. Sherman, *Sherman's Civil War*, 755, 758.

CHAPTER THREE

"OUR CAUSE IS NOT LOST"
The Confederate Response

AS SHERMAN PREPARED for a campaign that would break the will of Southerners, the Confederate army in Georgia regrouped. After evacuating Atlanta, John Bell Hood moved his men into camps about 30 miles away, waiting to see what would happen next. There was no fighting, for the Rebel army was in no condition to renew the contest. The previous four months had taken a toll on both sides, but it had hit the South harder, since the Confederacy had no way to replace men and matériel. The Confederates had lost almost fifty pieces of artillery and more than 13,000 small arms in their unsuccessful effort to hold on to Atlanta. Moreover, the arsenals at Augusta and Macon were struggling to produce needed ammunition for both cannons and muskets. Even more important than the shortage of weapons was the sinking morale; wounded men filled the hospitals, and desertions increased daily, for the loss of Atlanta was symptomatic of the mounting troubles facing the Confederacy.[1]

To boost the soldiers' spirits, Confederate president Jefferson Davis headed west to meet with Hood and the men in the Army of Tennessee. He also intended to talk with civilians along the route to remind them that the nation still needed their support. Georgia, he knew, was going to be a real test of his powers of persuasion. With Sherman in Atlanta, residents of Macon and Augusta, both sites of important munition factories, nervously awaited assurances that the Confederacy would not abandon them in the face of the enemy.

Before the war, Georgia had been one of the most prosperous states below the Mason-Dixon line and had earned a reputation as the "Empire State of the South." Its close to 60,000 square miles made it the largest state east of the Mississippi River, and its more than 1,000,000 inhabitants ranked it third in population of the eleven states that joined the Confederacy. Although about 44 percent of that number were slaves, some 20,000 white farmers were landless laborers; in the north Georgia mountains, farms were small and

John Bell Hood (Library of Congress)

slaveowners rare. Most of the state's slaves could be found in the black belt located across the center of the state and along the coast; the wealthiest 25 percent of the population owned more than 80 percent of the slaves.[2]

Many Georgians had not wanted a war. In the presidential election of 1860, when voters turned out in record numbers, they gave the two moderate candidates, Stephen A. Douglas and John Bell, almost 54,500 votes, whereas the Southern Democrat, John C. Breckinridge, earned fewer than 52,000. Without a clear winner, the election had been thrown into the state legislature, and all ten electoral votes went for Breckinridge. The following January, Georgia became the fifth state to secede despite the opposition of such men as Alexander Stephens, Linton Stephens, Benjamin H. Hill, and Herschel V. Johnson. The Radicals—including Howell Cobb, who had resigned as U.S. secretary of the treasury to throw his support behind secession; his brother Thomas R. R. Cobb; and Georgia's Senator Robert Toombs, a states' rights Democrat—won, and the ordinance of secession passed by a vote of 208 to 89. When the news spread, celebrations broke out among secessionists across the state. In Savannah the booming of more than 100 cannon could be heard throughout the city.[3]

One of those to support secession was Georgia's controversial governor, Joseph E. Brown, who was forty years old in the first year of the war. Although born in South Carolina, Brown had been raised in north Georgia and drew his support from small upland farmers. A graduate of Yale Law School, he had been a member of the Georgia bar, served one term in the state legislature, and sat as a judge before being elected governor in 1857. His popularity with the common people gave him a fourth two-year term in November 1863 by a vote of 36,558 of some 65,000 cast.[4]

Brown had a troubled relationship with the Confederate government, however. His extreme states' rights stand meant that he did not always cooperate with the central government in Richmond. In 1862, calling the conscription act unconstitutional and despotic, he created his own state militia; throughout the war he reorganized it to mirror changes in draft laws in order to keep a defensive force within the state. The governor proved particularly protective of his militia officers, shielding them so consistently from conscription that they were soon known as "Joe Brown's Pets." In June 1864, as Sherman pushed toward Atlanta, one of Howell Cobb's sons wrote, "Joe Brown is in Atlanta with his pets the militia officers and says he will lead them in the fight when the time comes. I hope the time will soon come, and that his time may come at the same time. I think his death would be a blessing to the country."[5]

Though not popular with everyone, Brown did win the allegiance of Georgia farmers. His primary concern was the state and its people, a stance that understandably played well with many voters. He worked to raise money for the relief of families whose husbands and fathers served in the army. He taxed the wealthy, including the state-owned railroad, and even hit the net income of speculators. Some argued that Brown was trying to start a class war, even though Georgia's businessmen and entrepreneurs likewise benefited from the booming economy.

With Atlanta under Union occupation in the autumn of 1864, successful Georgians pondered the future. Besides Atlanta, the cities of Columbus, Augusta, and Macon had flourished as military-industrial centers in the first three years of fighting, and entrepreneurs worried that whatever Sherman chose to do next had the potential of causing significant damage in the Confederacy's industrial heart. Columbus, on the Chattahoochee River in western Georgia, seemed one likely target. Although refugees had since enlarged the population, in 1860 Columbus had 5,965 whites and 3,656 blacks. An important manufacturing center, it hosted the largest sword factory in the South. Moreover, the Confederate navy used the old Columbus Iron Works to build ships and artillery.[6]

In eastern Georgia the Augusta Powder Works, one of the most important sites in the South, was another likely military objective. Trains running to Charleston and Columbia, South Carolina, carried ammunition, powder, cannon, and all kinds of military goods to Lee's army in Virginia. Augusta in 1860 had claimed a population of 8,495 whites and 3,998 blacks. The city had so far been untouched by the fighting, as a visitor from abroad noted in June 1863: "No place that I have seen in the Southern States shows so little traces of the war, and it formed a delightful contrast to the warworn, poverty-stricken, dried-up towns I had lately visited."[7]

Sherman could turn west toward Columbus or east to Augusta, but Georgians in the state's interior also worried. In central Georgia, Macon hosted an arsenal that manufactured cannon, shot, shells, and other needed ordnance. In 1860, Macon had been the state's fifth largest city, with 5,361 whites and 2,886 blacks. Columbus, Augusta, and Macon typified a state where industrialists had prospered in the prewar years. Indeed, on the eve of the Civil War, *DeBow's Review* had boasted, "Is there a State in Christendom in the enjoyment of so many material elements of comfort, prosperity and success as the great state of Georgia? . . . That day shall come

[when] . . . Georgia will not only be the Empire State of the South, but the Empire State of the World."[8]

A central route would also take Sherman toward Andersonville, site of the notorious Confederate prison. The compound, named Camp Sumter, originally covered about 16 acres, but 10 additional acres had been added to handle the increasing numbers as the war brought more prisoners. Before the camp shut down, some 45,000 men marched through the gates and attempted to endure the unhealthy conditions that came from having too many men in too small a space. In August 1864, just before Sherman took Atlanta, Andersonville held its highest number: about 33,000 inmates were living in primitive shelters and utilizing the one sluggish stream that ran through the middle of the stockade for both drinking water and waste disposal. The Confederacy did not furnish clothing, and huts were in short supply; men wore what they had on when they arrived, and latecomers lived in holes dug in the ground. Sickness was common. During fourteen months of operation, almost 13,000 prisoners died. Poor diet and inadequate medical attention meant that numerous men succumbed daily to scurvy, dysentery, diarrhea, and a variety of infections. So in September, Georgians below Macon also watched Sherman carefully, for liberating the prisoners at Andersonville seemed a logical goal for the Union army.

When President Davis arrived in Georgia just over three weeks after the Confederates surrendered Atlanta, he faced several difficult tasks. One immediate concern was the necessity to work out differences within the army command system, always a problem with the contentious officer corps in the Army of Tennessee. Davis also had to bolster morale among both soldiers and civilians. Most important, he needed to discuss strategy with Hood. Georgians placed their trust in the president; they had to believe that he had a plan. No one wanted to think that he would abandon the state and its people. "Our cause is not lost," he announced to an anxious audience in Macon. "Sherman cannot keep up his long line of communication; and retreat sooner or later he must. And when that day comes, the fate that befell the army of the French Empire in its retreat from Moscow will be reenacted." Moreover, he declared, as the son of a Georgian, "[I would be] untrue to myself if I should forget the State in her day of peril."[9]

Northerners read newspaper accounts of Davis's speeches, and when Grant saw the comment about Napoleon, he quipped: "Mr. Davis has not made it quite plain who is to furnish the snow for this Moscow retreat through Georgia and Tennessee. However, he has rendered us one good service at least in notifying us of Hood's intended plan of campaign." Sherman later wrote: "To be forewarned was to be forearmed," and the *New York Herald* even reported, "Old Abe will chuckle over this Macon speech as something more refreshing than a joke, and Grant and Sherman will find in it more useful information than could be gathered by all the scouts of the Union armies in a month." In fact, Davis revealed no strategy that Sherman had not already figured out for himself, but the Northern press enjoyed ridiculing the Confederate president.[10]

Davis's visit also drew attention in Washington. After the fall of Atlanta, Sherman had told Lincoln that he might be able to negotiate with Governor Brown, who was unhappy with the Richmond government, and perhaps even persuade Brown to bring Georgia back into the Union. Through negotiations undertaken by some former congressmen, the general promised Brown that if he would withdraw the state's quota from the Confederate army and help expel the Rebels from Georgia, then the march through the state would not desolate the land; Sherman would keep his men "to the high roads and commons and pay for the corn and meat we need and take." Sherman thought that Vice President Alexander Stephens, who was "a Union man at heart," might also be willing to talk. He was wrong on both counts, for neither Brown nor Stephens showed any interest. When Sherman told Lincoln that Davis had arrived in Georgia, the U.S. president commented, "I judge that Brown and Stephens are the objects of his visit."[11]

Davis, in fact, had several objectives. One of the changes that he made was to relieve Lieutenant General William J. Hardee from command of a corps in Hood's army and reassign him to the Department of South Carolina, Georgia, and Florida. In reality, Davis did this to appease both Hood and Hardee, as the two men could not work together. But the decision was popular with civilians as well, since Hardee, who was a Georgian, would go to Savannah. Moreover, the 49-year-old general had enjoyed one of the most esteemed reputations in the old army. If anyone could protect Georgia, Hardee had all the qualifications. Upon announcing this decision to a crowd in Augusta, Davis declared, "Two of these gentlemen who crossed this floor with me you have cheered, and you have cheered them because you respect those who have freely ventured their lives in your defence. One is Georgia's own son— the hero of many hard-fought fields—your own good and true

Hardee (cheers). . . . The other—[P. G. T.] Beauregard—(cheers) goes to share the toils, the fortunes, the misfortunes, if it be so, of the army in Georgia."[12]

William J. Hardee (National Archives)

Davis's decision to bring Beauregard from Virginia was another significant change. Concern over the Western Theater had prompted the president to place Beauregard in command of the Military Division of the West, a new department that would include Richard

Taylor in Mississippi, Hood's army in Georgia, and Hardee's troops along the coast. This, too, was a popular decision. Beauregard was the hero of Fort Sumter. Even Robert E. Lee had told Davis: "Should you deem, therefore, a change in the commander of the army in Georgia advantageous, and select General Beauregard for that position, I think you may feel assured that he understands the general condition of affairs, the difficulties with which they are surrounded, and the importance of exerting all his energies for their improvement." Although Davis had not wanted to relieve Hood from command of the Army of Tennessee, he was willing to place Beauregard over him.[13]

Feeling that he had the situation in hand, the president returned to Richmond, confident that Hood, Hardee, and Beauregard would take care of Georgia. Hood and Davis had worked out a plan and, considering the circumstances, not a bad plan. It played on the fact that Hood's army was smaller and more mobile than Sherman's three armies. Hood's rolls on September 20 indicated around 36,000 soldiers and 3,700 officers, although probably only some 33,000 infantry and artillery were available. Sherman's soldiers and animals needed far greater amounts of supplies and fodder. (Sherman admitted that he had his "wedge pretty deep, and must look out that I don't get my fingers pinched.") If Hood could hit the rail line, Sherman, forced to protect his communications, might be tempted out of Atlanta, thus relinquishing the city he had recently gained. In this way the Confederates would also draw the Union army away from the industrial centers at Columbus, Macon, and Augusta. Hood had already asked Davis to remove the Federal prisoners from Andersonville so that he would not have to worry about remaining between Sherman and the compound. In September, then, weary prisoners of war had been transferred to Camp Lawton at Millen, a small town on the railroad between Augusta and Savannah. It was hardly an improvement. Noted one Union captive, the men "died from exposure, as not more than half of us have any shelter but a ragged blanket propped upon sticks, under which the rain drizzles through like spray, completely wetting the occupants before many hours. . . . Disease and starvation together are decimating us daily, and the average deaths are twenty to thirty-five per day."[14]

With the Andersonville stockade emptied, Hood moved his army north just days after Davis left the state. A Confederate soldier wrote his wife that the Rebels had "gained a position in Sherman's rear, by one of the boldest flank movements on record." The goal, he added, was *"to compel Sherman to evacuate Atlanta.* In that case, he will either have to come out & fight us on our own ground, or attempt to make his way South. Whichever 'horn of the dilemmas' he may take hold of, we feel pretty sure that before the close of the campaign his army will be routed & driven back, if not totally destroyed—that is, provided no untoward event happens to prevent the success of our present plan of operations." Somewhat prophetically, he added, "A failure would be disastrous to us in the extreme."[15]

Having no choice but to follow Hood, Sherman left a corps to hold Atlanta and tracked the Rebel army. This was annoying, of course, because it meant postponing his own preparations. In any case, though, Lincoln had made it clear that he did not support Sherman striking out across uncharted territory until after the presidential election in November, telling the secretary of war that a "misstep" by Sherman "might be fatal to his army" and, by extension, to Lincoln's reelection. Grant had concurred when he wrote Sherman, "If there is any way of getting at Hood's army, I would prefer that," yet Grant indicated his confidence in Sherman as a strategist when he added, "but I must trust to your own judgment."[16]

In the meantime, Sherman used spies to find out what was going on in the Rebel cities. "I have ordered one of my female scouts from New Orleans to Augusta," he told Halleck in late September, "and will send some out from here and give you prompt notice of any of Hood's army going East." The woman, Mrs. N. W. Meyer, used the name of Nora Winder. Traveling with her 12-year-old son, she moved from Augusta to Milledgeville before heading for Savannah, along the route collecting information from Southern friends. She received money for expenses through Georgia Unionists. When she missed one of her contacts, Winder told the general, "I had to work my way a part of the time. Weaving pays well in the Confederacy, and I am a splendid weaver." Sometimes, lacking money, she and her son "had to walk; though if we had been riding we would have been suspected by the pickets, and as we were walking we were never suspected to be going farther than five or seven miles."[17]

Sherman did not need the help of spies to tell him that the Confederate army was on a raid. Hood's soldiers hit Big Shanty, Acworth, and Kennesaw, destroying the railroad track as they marched north. They could not hold what they took, so they kept moving, hoping to draw Sherman away from Atlanta. In the long run, there was little damage, for Union engineers could rebuild rail lines almost as quickly as the Rebels could dismantle them. Moreover, there was some Southern opposition to this strategy. General Joseph E. Johnston, a critic of Davis, pointed out that Hood's "movement has uncovered the route (thro' Macon) by which the army of Virginia is supplied, and the shops at which ammunition is prepared and arms repaired for the Army of Tennessee. If Sherman understands that either Charleston, Savannah, Pensacola or Mobile is as good a point for him as Chattanooga, he will not regard Hood's move."[18]

Sherman, who would have preferred to disregard the Rebel raid, on October 11 pushed for permission to break off from Hood and turn south. "Instead of being on the defensive, I would be on the offensive; instead of guessing at what he means to do, he would have to guess at my plans," he told Grant. "The difference in war is full 25 per cent. I can make Savannah, Charleston, or the mouth of the Chattahoochee. Answer quick, as I know we will not have the telegraph long."[19]

He was right; the Rebels did cut his communications. The cavalry under Joseph Wheeler had rejoined the army, hitting the railroad and telegraph lines north of Atlanta. At the same time, Rebel horsemen attacked the lines in Tennessee. Sherman complained to Grant that it was "a physical impossibility to protect the roads, now that Hood, Forrest, and Wheeler, and the whole batch of devils, are turned loose without home or habitation." He pointed out that the destruction of 8 miles of track required huge quantities of iron, new ties, and thousands of men to repair.[20]

Clearly, the Rebels had caused havoc. Although Grant answered Sherman on October 11, writing, "If you are satisfied the trip to the sea-coast can be made, holding the line of the Tennessee firmly, you may make it," it was days before Sherman received the message. Moreover, Horace Porter, who served as Grant's aide-de-camp, later wrote that Sherman claimed a November 2 date as the "first time General Grant ordered the march to the sea." Nonetheless, whenever it was that Grant approved the march, it was the permission that Sherman had been waiting for.[21]

In the meantime, those suffering shortages were the civilians remaining in Atlanta and north Georgia. Foraging increased in the countryside when the railroad could no longer provide enough food for the hungry Union soldiers and fodder for the animals. Foraging parties scavenged the farms and plantations for anything to eat. One Northern soldier tried to reassure his family that what they did was necessary when he wrote, "It may seem barbarous to you to rob henroosts but Hood cut off our R R communication and forced us to forage for corn & of course we don't refuse to accept any thing better that offers. All is fair in war you know."[22] Union soldiers generally made light of the foraging, however. One Connecticut soldier reported that "raiding parties are all the rage with us yet." When a group returned to camp with all kind of vegetables, livestock, pigs, and chickens, the men had "more potatoes & fowl so we live like epicures. I never ate so many sweet potatoes in one week as in the past one, and they agree with my taste and constitution too to a charm. We have a bushel or more yet for us three."[23]

Georgians understood what fate awaited them if the Yankees came to visit. Thomas Maguire, whose plantation called Promised Land was near the Gwinnett-DeKalb county line, tried to protect what little he had. As raiding parties scoured the countryside, he wrote on October 19, "This day devoted to hiding out wheat, two boxes in the farmer field, 80 bushels. Little hands pulling fodder of syrup-cane in the patches. Will put out some barrels of syrup this day making preparation for the evil time coming should it come." Nevertheless, when Union troops did arrive, they took everything, and on November 3, Maguire lamented, "What will become of us. God only knows."[24]

Davis had hoped that he could protect most of Georgia by having Hood follow the Western & Atlantic, drawing Sherman out of the city and forcing him to battle. The president had also arranged for Alabama militia to move from Montgomery through Gadsden to Augusta, with the intention of providing additional protection for the powder works. He thought it might even be necessary for Hood to cover Augusta. Although Davis still hoped for a "conclusive battle" that would be the turning point in the Western Theater, he agreed that Hood could fall back into Alabama and draw his supplies from Richard Taylor's department. This plan, Davis later pointed out, could "rescue Georgia, save the Gulf States, and retain possession of the lines of communication upon which we depended."[25]

The whole situation frustrated Sherman. "I cannot guess his movements as I could those of Johnston, who was a sensible man and only did sensible things," he complained. "If Hood does not mind I will catch him yet in a worse snap than he has been in." He

finally declared that if Hood wanted to "go to the Ohio River I will
give him rations. Let him go north. My business is down South."[26]
Hood, who was constantly revising his plan as he tried to outfox
Sherman, apparently hoped that the Federals would weaken as they
detached men to guard the railroad. He told Richmond on October
8 that destroying Sherman's communications would force him "to
fall back or move south. If the latter, I shall move on his rear; if the
former, I shall move to the Tennessee River via La Fayette and
Gadsden."[27]

Such vague words could hardly have assured the Confederate
government, and even as he wrote these words, assuring Braxton
Bragg that he would follow Sherman's trail, Hood had already considered other options. He no longer wanted to tempt Sherman into
battle somewhere on the railroad north of Atlanta or, apparently,
to lure Sherman into Alabama in order to fight there. Nor did his
message make clear what he intended to do if he did move to the
Tennessee River, and it certainly did not seem to take into account
the safety of Georgia. Moreover, he had decided to deviate from
the plan that he and Davis had agreed upon during the president's
visit. Perhaps Hood did not think that Georgians needed any help.
Beauregard, on his way to join Hood's army at Cave Spring, a resort in the mountains near the Alabama border, had stopped in
Milledgeville to talk with Governor Brown. Georgia's chief executive had assured the general that he could raise 30,000 men, but
even that number would not be enough to stop Sherman's veterans. Both Hood and Beauregard should have recognized that Brown
could not protect Georgia alone, but unfortunately for Georgians,
these two important men had trouble communicating. Perhaps
Beauregard, who had not yet officially assumed command of the
Military Division of the West, did not feel he could supersede Hood
until he had the authority. It is also possible that Beauregard simply had no other idea and just decided to let Hood take the initiative. Whatever the reason, Beauregard did nothing to stop Hood
from heading his army into Alabama and leaving Governor Brown
to deal with Sherman.

Not everyone approved of the decision to move away from
Sherman. "The policy of taking advantage of the reported division
of Sherman's forces by attacking him where (or *when*) he cannot
reunite his army is too obvious to have been overlooked by you,"
President Davis wrote Hood on November 7. "I therefore take it
for granted that you have not been able to avail yourself of that

advantage during his march northward from Atlanta, and hope the opportunity will be offered before he is extensively recruited." Of course, if Sherman moved the main army south, "you may first beat him in detail and subsequently without serious obstruction or danger to the country in your rear advance to the Ohio River." Focusing only on the last few words, Hood took them as Richmond's approval for his decision to march into Tennessee.[28]

During October, Hood had befuddled Sherman. He had drawn Union forces out of Atlanta and assumed the initiative, thus setting the Northern press on fire with warnings that the Rebels might rebound from the city's loss. Sherman's response, as one historian observed, was dismal: he had "trailed in his enemy's wake until he had been drawn over a hundred miles back from Atlanta." It was Sherman's own fault that the Confederate army had regrouped; according to one authority, the fact that Sherman had not attacked the wounded Confederate army after capturing Atlanta was a "cardinal mistake." Another student of military tactics and strategy called it probably the "greatest mistake of his military career." Sherman, of course, explained of his wily opponent, "Hood can turn and twist like a fox."[29]

Even though Hood had succeeded in leading Sherman on a chase through northern Georgia, he elected not to bring the army to battle. When he turned west for Alabama, eventually marching into Tennessee, he intended to strike for Nashville before a Union presence could oppose him there; with luck he thought he could plant his banner on the banks of the Ohio River. Had Hood's Tennessee campaign worked out differently, Sherman certainly would have been forced to suspend his march to the sea and return to fight the Confederate army. As John Schofield, who faced Hood in Tennessee, noted after the war, "The fortune of war was on the whole always in my favour." Although this may be an overstatement, since Schofield barely escaped from Hood at Spring Hill on November 29, it does hold a modicum of truth. Colonel Henry Stone rather grandly concluded, "Hood conceived and entered upon a campaign, unsurpassed for boldness, and, so long as pitted against Sherman, for success, by any undertaken by any Confederate General during the whole four years struggle." Georgians, of course, would not agree, and campaigns are remembered by their success or failure. With Hood's failure, the entire Confederacy suffered.[30]

While Hood framed his strategy, Sherman lobbied Grant. "I propose we break up the railroad from Chattanooga, and strike out with wagons for Milledgeville, Millen, and Savannah. . . . By attempting to hold the [rail]roads we will lose 1,000 men monthly, and will gain no result. . . . We have over 8,000 cattle and 3,000,000 of bread, but no corn; but we can forage in the interior of the State." (Indeed, one of Sherman's generals complained that same day, "I feel very anxious to send out a strong foraging party as soon as you deem it prudent. We need forage. I have not a pound for my own private horse, and all our animals have been out several days.") Moreover, Sherman observed when he abandoned Atlanta, he intended "to ruin Georgia." He wanted to show that "war and individual ruin are synonymous terms."[31]

Sherman had based his argument on the belief that following the Rebels made no sense. He told one of his generals that Hood's "whole movement is inexplicable to any common sense theory." It was also true that warfare had evolved over the three years of fighting. Cities were no longer the targets they had been early in the war, and in Virginia the cry "On to Richmond" had been replaced by the goal of destroying Lee's army. Using towns or space on the map as objectives was a strategy of commanders in earlier wars and in the early years of the Civil War. Thus, to some observers, Sherman was backsliding by not destroying Hood's army.[32]

One Union observer, Major General Joseph Hooker, used Sherman's plan to march away from the Confederate army as an excuse to criticize the general. From a desk in Cincinnati, Hooker blamed Grant and Sherman for his lack of a field command and took every opportunity to grumble. "Had Sherman marched against Hood, there was no earthly reason why he should escape," he noted on December 8. "Sherman is crazy," he declared, "he has no more judgment than a child." To Benjamin F. Wade, an influential Radical Republican, he wrote, "No matter what the newspapers may say to the contrary, no officer high in command has been more unfortunate than Sherman, and this moment he is engaged in a raid which will tend to prolong the war, when he had it in his power to have utterly destroyed Hood's army." Hooker vented his anger at Sherman by adding: "At the time he cut loose from Atlanta, Hood was on the north side of the Tennessee River, but instead of marching for him, he chose to march from him. Blows, not marches, are to kill the rebellion."[33]

Sherman, of course, disagreed. If his strategy worked out as planned, it would be his march, not a battle, that would end the rebellion.

NOTES

1. Thomas Lawrence Connelly, *Autumn of Glory: The Army of Tennessee, 1862–1865* (Baton Rouge: Louisiana State University Press, 1971), 468; *O.R.* 38, pt. 1, 124–26.

2. Only 3,594 farms had 500 to 1,000 acres under cultivation; only twenty-three Georgians owned more than 200 slaves, and only one person owned more than 1,000 slaves. Anne J. Bailey and Walter J. Fraser, *Portraits of Conflict: A Photographic History of Georgia in the Civil War* (Fayetteville: University of Arkansas Press, 1996), 27.

3. In 1860, Georgia had a population of 591,550 whites, 462,198 slaves, and some 3,500 free persons of color. Bell won 42,886 in the election, Douglas only 11,580. On January 2, Georgians had voted 50,243 to 37,123 to hold a secession convention. Anne J. Bailey, "Georgia," in Archie P. McDonald, ed., *A Nation of Sovereign States: Secession and War in the Confederacy* (Murfreesboro, TN: Southern Heritage Press, 1994), 69–71.

4. Ibid., 73.

5. Ibid. Earlier in the war, Brown had fielded an army composed entirely of militia officers to protect Savannah, but the officers in Atlanta in 1864 were on hand to lead a newly organized division of militiamen. I. W. Avery, *History of the State of Georgia from 1850 to 1881* (New York: Brown & Derby, 1881), 256–57.

6. For the statistics, see Bailey and Fraser, *Portraits of Conflict*, 28. For more on Columbus, see Stewart C. Edwards, " 'To do the Manufacturing for the South': Private Industry in Confederate Columbus," *Georgia Historical Quarterly* 85 (Winter 2001): 538–54.

7. Arthur J. L. Fremantle, *Three Months in the Southern States, April–June 1863* (Edinburgh: William Blackwood & Sons, 1863), 176. For the statistics, see Bailey and Fraser, *Portraits of Conflict*, 28.

8. Mary A. DeCredico, *Patriotism for Profit: Georgia's Urban Entrepreneurs and the Confederate War Effort* (Chapel Hill: University of North Carolina Press, 1990), 13. For the statistics, see Bailey and Fraser, *Portraits of Conflict*, 28.

9. Jefferson Davis, *Jefferson Davis, Constitutionalist: His Letters, Papers, and Speeches*, 8 vols., ed. Dunbar Rowland (Jackson: Mississippi Department of Archives and History, 1923), 6:356–61.

10. Horace Porter, *Campaigning with Grant* (New York: The Century Co., 1897), 313; Sherman, *Memoirs*, 2:141; Davis, *Jefferson Davis, Constitutionalist*, 6:353, 358; *New York Herald*, October 8, 1864.

11. *O.R.* 39, pt. 2, 396, 488; Sherman, *Memoirs*, 2:138–39.

12. Mark M. Boatner III, *The Civil War Dictionary* (New York: David McKay Co., Inc., 1959), 374; Ezra J. Warner, *Generals in Gray: Lives of the Confederate Commanders* (Baton Rouge: Louisiana State University Press, 1959), 124–25; Nathaniel Cheairs Hughes Jr., "William J. Hardee," in Current, *Encyclopedia of the Confederacy*, 2:737–38; Richard M. McMurry, "William Joseph Hardee," in William C. Davis, ed., *The Confederate Generals*, 6 vols. (Harrisburg, PA: National Historical Society, 1991), 3:58–61.

13. *O.R.* 39, pt. 2, 846.

14. Herman Hattaway and Archer Jones, *How the North Won: A Military History of the Civil War* (Urbana: University of Illinois Press, 1983), 633; diary entry dated November 1, 1864, in Sneden, *Eye of the Storm*, 261.

15. Letter of James Madison Brannock dated October 5, 1864, Sarah Caroline (Gwin) Brannock Collection, Virginia Historical Society, Richmond.

16. *O.R.* 39, pt. 3, 202, 222; Sherman, *Memoirs*, 2:152–53.

17. *O.R.* 39, pt. 2, 404; 47, pt. 2, 396–97. According to Brigadier General William P. Carlin, Sherman would see one of his female spies in Milledgeville. See Carlin, *Memoirs*, 152.

18. Hattaway and Jones, *How the North Won*, 631.

19. *O.R.* 39, pt. 3, 202.

20. Ibid., 162; Wiley Sword, *The Confederacy's Last Hurrah: Spring Hill, Franklin, and Nashville* (1992; reprint, Lawrence: University Press of Kansas, 1993), 59.

21. *O.R.* 39, pt. 3, 202; Porter, *Campaigning with Grant*, 317–18.

22. Letter dated October 22, 1864, in James A. Padgett, ed., "With Sherman through Georgia and the Carolinas: Letters of a Federal Soldier," *Georgia Historical Quarterly* 33 (March 1949): 49; Garrett, *Atlanta*, 1:647–48.

23. Letter dated October 29, 1864, in Padgett, "Letters of a Federal Soldier," 51; Garrett, *Atlanta*, 1:647.

24. Garrett, *Atlanta*, 1:648.

25. Davis, *Jefferson Davis, Constitutionalist*, 2:565, 6:353, 8:415.

26. *O.R.* 39, pt. 3, 135; Steven E. Woodworth, *Jefferson Davis and His Generals: The Failure of Confederate Command in the West* (Lawrence: University Press of Kansas, 1990), 294.

27. *O.R.* 39, pt. 3, 804–5.

28. Davis, *Jefferson Davis, Constitutionalist*, 6:399.

29. The quotations are from Sherman's biographer Liddell Hart, historian T. R. Hay, and historian Alfred H. Burne, all found in Burne, *Lee, Grant, and Sherman*, 137–38.

30. Ibid., 143–44.

31. *O.R.* 39, pt. 3, 162–63, 359, 378.

32. Ibid., 177.

33. *O.R.* 45, pt. 2, 111–12.

CHAPTER FOUR

"JOHN BROWN'S SOUL GOES MARCHING ON"
Sherman Leaves Atlanta

ONE WEEK AFTER the presidential election, Sherman's wagons rolled out of Atlanta. He ordered all the buildings that might be useful to the Confederates demolished and all military supplies burned, but the flames spread to houses in the downtown, and it was impossible to halt the destruction. One Northern officer noted that a brigade of New England soldiers was the last to leave, and as the columns marched out of the city, he had listened to "the really fine band of the Thirty-third Massachusetts playing 'John Brown's soul goes marching on,' by the light of the burning buildings. I have never heard that noble anthem when it was so grand, so solemn, so inspiring." Even Sherman noted that he had "never before or since . . . heard the chorus of 'Glory, glory, hallelujah!' done with more spirit, or in better harmony of time and place."[1]

Sherman's intention of crushing Atlanta's military usefulness was thoroughly realized. When Governor Brown ordered W. P. Howard to survey what was left of Atlanta after Sherman had gone, he learned that the railroad depot, car shed, machine shops, foundries, rolling mills, merchant mills, arsenals, armory, and other industrial property had burned. Even the jail and all the hotels, except the Gate City, had gone up in flames. Moreover, two-thirds of the shade trees had been cut down to provide firewood and building material. "Atlanta, the beautiful, the 'Gate City' is dead," a departing Federal soldier had observed.[2]

To make matters worse, pillagers still roamed the streets when Howard arrived some three weeks after Sherman's departure. He estimated 250 wagons loaded with plunder including, "pianoes, mirrors, furniture of all kinds, iron, hides without number, and an incalculable amount of other things, very valuable at the present time." As if the Yankees had not proved enough of a threat, bushwhackers, robbers, deserters, and a few loyal Confederates from the surrounding country had "been engaged in this dirty work." Even the suburbs "present to the eye one vast, naked, ruined, deserted camp." Two to three thousand dead animals lay rotting in the sun. In the cemeteries, where cavalrymen had allowed their horses to graze, "the ornaments of graves, such as marble lambs, miniature statuary, souvenirs of departed little ones are broken and scattered abroad." As a final insult, Howard claimed that bodies had been removed from vaults in the cemetery in order to get at the silver nameplates and tippings. Although he also asserted that Yankee dead had replaced the exhumed corpses, that story seems unlikely.[3]

In fact, it was unnecessary to exaggerate the damage. Sherman had indeed accomplished what he intended: he had destroyed the capability of the Confederates to use the city as a post in his rear. On December 22, after Sherman was safely at Savannah, the *Atlanta Daily Intelligencer* reported, "No whistle from railroad engines, no crowing of cocks, no grunting of hogs, no braying of mules, no lowing of cows, no whirring of machinery, no sound of hammer and saw—nothing but the howling of dogs was heard in our midst." A correspondent for the Augusta paper noted that "thousands of cats and dogs, ownerless and almost wild" prowled Atlanta's streets.[4]

Civilians who read these accounts worried about what would happen if the Union hordes came their way. Georgians feared for their lives as well as their property. This result was what the general intended, for the psychological effects of such anxieties could be as draining as the actual event; Sherman did not have to devastate the landscape to evoke a terrified response. One Atlanta woman wrote her brother, who was a soldier in Lee's Army of Northern Virginia, "I hadn't undressed to go to bed in a month until last night. . . . The whole country is full of dead horses and mules, and the ditches standing full of stagnant water, enough to kill anything." Still, she was optimistic: "We are making our calculations to live rather hard next year," she added. "But if we can live at all, I am not afraid that we will perish."[5]

The Union men who left behind such chaos had marched out of Atlanta just as confident as their commander. One soldier, caught up in the devil-may-care exhilaration of the moment, even shouted to his commander, "Uncle Billy, I guess Grant is waiting for us at Richmond!" Yet in spite of a united goal to destroy the Confederacy, the men's motives varied greatly. Some soldiers wanted to march for the freedom of the slaves. Others wanted to cross Georgia to show Confederates that Southern rights could not prevail. A few simply wanted to get even with someone (and anyone would do) for all the hardships and heartaches the war had brought. They knew that Hood had headed west and did not expect him to be a problem, but they did not know what response the Confederate government might have planned for them. Rumors abounded that Joseph E. Johnston, their old nemesis from the Atlanta campaign, might bring an army to Georgia. Some even thought that Braxton Bragg, their foe from earlier days, could return to block their march.[6]

Sherman understood that if the campaign succeeded, it would be considered just "a matter of course," whereas if he failed, the march "would be adjudged the wild adventure of a crazy fool." Therefore, the two wings headed in different directions, both to assure forage for the men and animals and to prevent an enemy concentration in their path. The right turned toward Griffin and Forsyth, in the direction of Macon, while the left moved on Decatur, toward Augusta. Unusually cold weather resulted in extensive destruction of fences and barns as the army progressed. "We would have frozen," wrote a soldier, "if the fence on both sides of our route had not been fired and burned by those ahead of us." After the left wing passed the huge granite outcropping known as Stone Mountain, soldiers burned the railroad depot and other property at Lithonia. A captain recalled that "food in gardens, food in cellars, stock in fields, stock in barns, poultry everywhere, appears in the distance, disappears in the presence, and was borne away upon the knapsacks and bayonets of thousands of soldiers." At Covington the color-bearers unfurled the Stars and Stripes, and the bands played Northern tunes. "The white people came out of their houses to behold the sight, [in] spite of their deep hatred of the invaders," later wrote Sherman, "and the negroes were simply frantic with joy." He declined an invitation to dine with the family of a former West Point classmate.[7]

Moving into the town of Social Circle, soldiers burned the railroad depot but not private residences; around fifty antebellum homes still exist there, and in prosperous Madison to the east, imposing homes still testify to the prewar wealth of the residents. In 1845 a visitor had described Madison as "the wealthiest and most aristocratic village on the stagecoach route between Charleston and New Orleans." One popular story claims that Joshua Hill, Union sympathizer and former U.S. senator, spoke personally to General

Slocum and asked him to spare the town. Hill had met Sherman during the Atlanta campaign when he had visited the general to request permission to retrieve the body of his son, who had been killed fighting the Federals near Cassville. He had told Sherman he was a friend of John Sherman, the general's brother. The two men had talked about the situation, and Hill had admitted that "further resistance on the part of the South was madness"; he hoped that the governor would "withdraw his people from the rebellion." Sherman had responded that if Brown would do so, he would "spare the State."[8]

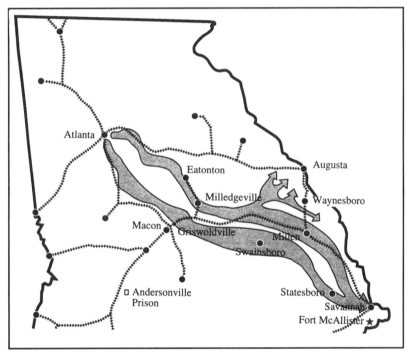

The left wing moved in the direction of Augusta and the right wing marched toward Macon, but Savannah was Sherman's objective.

Although the elegant homes of Madison remained untouched, the railroad depot was burned and the business area sacked. Moreover, each farm, plantation, and village along the route endured similar treatment. Rarely were the homes in the larger towns touched, but soldiers plundered smokehouses, took all the flour, cornmeal, fruits, and vegetables. They confiscated or killed the horses, mules, cattle, hogs, and chickens, leaving only scraps for the people to eat. A careful study of the census for Georgia's counties had given Sherman a good idea of which regions could support his hungry men and animals. Since the two wings were separated by twenty to forty miles, nothing in their path escaped. Even Sherman admitted, "No doubt, many acts of pillage, robbery, and violence, were committed by these parties of foragers, usually called 'bummers,' for I have since heard of jewelry taken from women, and the plunder of articles that never reached the commissary; but these acts were exceptional and incidental," and "this system of foraging was simply indispensable to our success."[9]

The only recorded acts of violence occurred when there was resistance. The Richmond government had urged Georgians to adopt a scorched-earth policy, and Beauregard had declared: "Arise, for the defense of your native soil: rally around your patriotic Governor and gallant soldiers. Obstruct and destroy all roads in Sherman's flanks and rear, and his army will soon starve. Be confident and resolute. Trust in an overruling providence, and success will crown your efforts." Governor Brown called for men between the ages of sixteen and fifty-five years to protect their homes. "Let every man fly to arms," wrote one prominent Georgian, "remove your negroes, horses, cattle and provisions away from Sherman's army and burn what you cannot carry, burn all bridges and block up the roads in his route." Of course, few Georgians actually took such measures, for to do so could mean wasting their homes.[10]

Some wealthy plantation owners did remove their slaves, but most did not, and scores of blacks flocked to the protection of the Union army. "Hundreds of slaves joined the Army," observed one soldier, "some with a half a dozen children along with them." No one tried to stop the exodus of the former bondsmen, and some soldiers privately enjoyed having black refugees carry their knapsacks. All the slaves were eager to please and offered to do menial tasks for their liberators.[11]

Most soldiers assumed that Macon and Augusta were their objectives because they were widely known to be industrial centers. The Confederate administration understood that also and had therefore ordered commanders to both posts. Braxton Bragg headed for Augusta (albeit without the army that Northerners thought he might raise), and Richard Taylor, Beauregard, and Hardee met in Macon. A soldier in the latter city wrote, "The times looks gloomy about here now, I assure you. The citizens of Macon are in great confusion and are moving out pretty fast."[12]

Union foragers leaving camp (*Harper's Weekly*)

Sherman's march was different from anything previously seen in the war. Even in the summer of 1863, when Grant partially abandoned his supply line at the Mississippi River and, living off the land, drove inland toward Jackson, Mississippi, there had been no overt plan to destroy the countryside. Many veterans now with Sherman had taken part in the Vicksburg campaign, yet even they sensed that this march across Georgia was somehow unique. They knew that part of the plan was to show Southerners that this could

Foragers killing livestock (*Leslie's Illustrated*)

be done and, by doing so, prove that the rebellion had failed. Macon, Augusta, Savannah, or even Charleston might fall, but crossing the heart of the Confederacy would have repercussions far beyond the actual physical damage.

The men whom Sherman chose for this task were a varied lot. The right-wing foot soldiers were almost entirely Midwesterners or Westerners, with infantrymen from Illinois outnumbering the other states, followed by those from Ohio, Iowa, Indiana, Missouri, Wisconsin, and a smattering from Michigan and Minnesota. In the left wing the largest number of infantrymen hailed from Ohio, with Illinois running second, followed by Indiana, Michigan, Wisconsin, and a few foot soldiers from Missouri and Minnesota. The obvious difference in the left wing, however, was the large number of New Yorkers and Pennsylvanians, plus a few men from Connecticut, Massachusetts, and New Jersey. In these units one could usually find a strongly opinionated abolitionist. Conversely and generally, men from the Midwest and West usually agreed with, and supported, Sherman's insistence on maintaining a white army.

Sherman had grown up in Ohio, a state that discouraged escaped slaves from remaining within its borders once the fugitives had made it safely across the Ohio River. He objected to the administration's decision to enlist black soldiers. "I prefer some negroes as pioneers, teamsters, cooks, and servants," he firmly declared in late July, "others gradually to experiment in the art of the Soldier, beginning with the duties of local garrison such as we had at Memphis, Vicksburg, Natchez—Nashville and Chattanooga." Lincoln disagreed, of course. A law in 1862 had provided for "colored" enlistments, and in 1863 the first black units actually took the field. It became a hotly debated matter, not only between Yankees and Rebels but between men in Lincoln's own government. Sherman, however, was the only military commander who continued to defy the president's wishes.[13]

Far from Washington, the president, and meddling administrators in the War Department, commanders in the Western Theater had always enjoyed more freedom of action than their counterparts in the East. Throughout the war, Sherman avoided making public comments on most political issues, but privately he was quite knowledgeable about what went on in Washington. In June 1862, Senator Sherman had told his brother that Lincoln was "honest & patriotic" but lacked "dignity, order & energy" and would fail at any business except "pettifogging." John even considered supporting a War Democrat in the 1864 election, writing that he would back almost anyone except "our Monkey President." The antiadministration press agreed, calling Lincoln a gorilla—even a black gorilla, for his decision to arm black men. Although General Sherman recognized that the demise of slavery foreshadowed change, he told his wife just months before the fighting ended that he still opposed blacks as soldiers. He had no objection to treating a black man "as free," but he did not think a former slave should be "hunted and badgered to make a soldier of, when his family is left back on the plantations. I am right and won't change."[14]

On the basis of his personal experiences in the South, Sherman concluded, "I think I understand the negro as well as anybody" and believe he "must pass through a probationary state before he is qualified for utter and complete freedom." The soldier issue was, therefore, an "open question" which, he admitted, "should be fairly and honestly tested." During the Atlanta campaign he had told Lorenzo Thomas, head of recruiting black soldiers along the Mississippi River, that he still thought former slaves best suited to be teamsters, pioneers, or servants; he had "no objection to the surplus, if any, being enlisted as soldiers, but I must have labor and a large quantity of it. I confess I would prefer 300 negroes armed with spades and axes than 1,000 as soldiers." And he told a recruiter, "I would not draw on the poor Race for too large a proportion of its active athletic Young men for some must remain to seek new homes and provide for the old and the young the feeble and helpless."[15]

He added that he liked blacks if they remained in their place, "but when fools and idiots [meaning white recruiters] try to make [them] better than ourselves, I have an opinion." He had even told Henry Halleck that a black man might be as good as a white man to stop a bullet, but "a sand-bag is better." Could they skirmish, do picket duty, and improvise when necessary? "I say no," he answered. Lincoln tactfully reminded the general that the law regarding black recruitment was "a law" and "must be treated as such by all of us."[16] Nevertheless, Sherman continued to ignore the president's wishes. He had told a recruiter that although some might say he had "peculiar notions" on the subject of blacks in combat, he was sure that those notions were "shared by a large portion of our fighting men." Clearly, one of his goals was to protect the morale of his soldiers, and he would oppose anyone, even his commander in chief, if that goal seemed endangered by integration. As events turned out, Sherman's capture of Atlanta made him a Northern hero and strengthened his position in the argument. He knew exactly how important the fall of Atlanta had been to the Republican Party: the Democrats, who had attacked Lincoln for the huge number of casualties in Grant's army in the early summer, could no longer claim that the war was a failure. Sherman continued to ignore Washington's pleas that he employ black soldiers in combat roles in his white armies.[17]

When Lincoln first approved black units, Sherman had written his wife, Ellen, that he could not bring himself to place black soldiers "with arms in positions of danger and trust." He even told his men that black recruits should not be brigaded with white men, but he assured his senator brother that he did not "object to the Government taking them from the Enemy, & making such use of them as experience may suggest." He conceded that he might one day change his opinion, but at that time he thought the army better served by blacks doing the manual labor that would then allow the white soldiers to win the war.[18]

Allowing slaves to follow his armies also diminished his ability to provide adequately for his veterans. Still, as the army reached the region of "rich planters," slaves fled their masters in ever increasing numbers, hoping to find freedom with the army in blue. One soldier observed, "It is most ludicrous to see the actions of the negro women as we pass. They seem to be half-crazy with joy, and when a band strikes up they go stark mad."[19]

Sherman's first problem, however, was not contrabands, as escaped slaves in Union hands were called; it was the weather. He had hoped to leave Atlanta after the autumn rains ended, but as the columns left the city, a cold drizzle fell. Moving wagons, artillery, thousands of horses and mules, and large cattle herds became a trial. Wagons bogged down and overturned, forcing men to shovel mud off into the ditch and roughen the underlying roadbed with picks or lay logs to provide traction. When overloaded wagons became mired and animals fell from exhaustion, they were left behind: the supplies were destroyed and the dying animals shot, leaving a clear trail of corpses. As the men marched, the continuing rain made it impossible to find dry wood for the fires needed for cooking and warmth. A cutting cold wind also made each step miserable. Sherman learned from the locals that this was one of the coldest Novembers in memory. When he camped for the night on November 21 and tried to warm himself with a drink of whiskey and a cigar, an old slave woman directed him to a dry place to sleep nearby: the double-hewed-log house of a local overseer on a plantation near Milledgeville.[20]

Sherman soon learned that he was on Hurricane Plantation, a few miles north of the state capital. The land and slaves belonged to Georgian Howell Cobb, a prewar governor and Democratic congressman who had initially spoken against secession but changed his tune after Lincoln's election. Cobb had served as chairman of the Montgomery convention in 1861 and as a general with the army in Virginia. He had returned to Georgia in 1863 to take command of the Georgia State Guard and now led the Confederate Reserves of Georgia. Sherman knew that Cobb had accompanied President Davis during his morale-boosting visit to the Army of Tennessee in late September. On the evening that Sherman camped on the plantation, Cobb was in Macon making plans to meet the Union advance. Since Sherman blamed men such as Cobb for the war, he instructed his soldiers to destroy everything except the cabins of the slaves.

On the afternoon of November 22, around 30,000 wet and muddy men marched into Milledgeville. Civilians watched the procession of Union blue and listened to the bands playing "The Battle Hymn of the Republic" as soldiers passed in front of the governor's mansion and the statehouse. Although most units camped across the Oconee River, east of the town, war had come to Georgia's capital city.[21]

NOTES

1. George Ward Nichols, *The Story of the Great March* (1865; reprint, Williamstown, MA: Corner House Publishers, 1972), 41; Sherman, *Memoirs*, 2:179.

2. *Macon Daily Telegraph and Confederate*, December 12, 1864; Cram, *Soldiering with Sherman*, 148.

3. *Macon Daily Telegraph and Confederate*, December 12, 1864.

4. *Atlanta Daily Intelligencer*, December 22, 1864; *Augusta Chronicle and Sentinel*, December 15, 1864.

5. "Lizzie's Letter," *Atlanta Journal Magazine*, April 23, 1944.

6. Sherman, *Memoirs*, 2:179.

7. Jim Miles, *To the Sea: A History and Tour Guide of Sherman's March* (Nashville: Rutledge Hill Press, 1989), 42–43; Sherman, *Memoirs*, 2:179–80.

8. Katharine M. Jones, comp., *When Sherman Came: Southern Women and the "Great March"* (New York: Bobbs-Merrill Co., 1964), 14; Sherman, *Memoirs*, 2:138.

9. Sherman, *Memoirs*, 2:182–83.

10. *Macon Daily Telegraph and Confederate*, November 18 and 21, 1864.
11. Miles, *To the Sea*, 61.
12. Lane, *"Dear Mother,"* 335.
13. Sherman, *Sherman's Civil War*, 678.
14. Michael Fellman, "Lincoln and Sherman" in Gabor S. Boritt, ed., *Lincoln's Generals* (New York: Oxford University Press, 1994), 127; Sherman, *Sherman's Civil War*, 798.
15. *O.R.* 39, pt. 2, 132; Sherman to John A. Spooner, July 30, 1864, enclosed in R. D. Mussey to Major [Charles W. Foster?], August 2, 1864, M-583 1864, Letters Received, ser. 360, Colored Troops Division, RG 94, Records of the Adjutant General's Office, National Archives, Washington, DC, quoted in Ira Berlin, Joseph P. Reidy, and Leslie S. Rowland, eds., *Freedom: A Documentary History of Emancipation, 1861–1867*, ser. 3; *The Black Military Experience* (New York: Cambridge University Press, 1982), 110–11. In spite of Sherman's evaluation of Georgia, at least 3,486 black Georgians and more than 2,300 white Georgians joined the Federal army; see Robert S. Davis Jr., "White and Black in Blue: The Recruitment of Federal Units in Civil War North Georgia," *Georgia Historical Quarterly* 55 (Fall 2001): 347–74.
16. Sherman to William M. McPherson, [c. September 1864], Sherman Papers, Huntington Library, San Marino, CA, quoted in Fellman, "Lincoln and Sherman," 146; *O.R.* 38, pt. 5, 793; *O.R.*, ser. 3, 4, 436 (same as June 20 letter); Abraham Lincoln to William T. Sherman, July 18, 1864, in *The Collected Works of Abraham Lincoln*, 9 vols., ed. Roy Basler (New Brunswick, NJ: Rutgers University Press, 1953), 7:449–50; Michael Fellman, *Citizen Sherman: A Life of William Tecumseh Sherman* (New York: Random House, 1995), 158–60. Lorenzo Thomas, who headed efforts to recruit black soldiers in the West, also told the secretary of war that he thought Sherman's threat to arrest recruiters was "especially harsh." *O.R.*, ser. 3, 4, 433–34.
17. Sherman to John A. Spooner, July 30, 1864; *O.R.*, ser. 3, 4, 789.
18. Sherman, *Sherman's Civil War*, 454, 461.
19. *Reminiscences of the Civil War from Diaries of Members of the 103d Illinois Volunteer Infantry* (Chicago: J. F. Leaming & Co., 1904), 148–49.
20. Sherman, *Memoirs*, 2:185.
21. James C. Bonner, "Sherman at Milledgeville in 1864," *Journal of Southern History* 22 (August 1956): 275.

CHAPTER FIVE

"LEAVING SUFFERING AND DESOLATION BEHIND THEM"

Milledgeville and Griswoldville

THE LITTLE TOWN of Milledgeville had become the official seat of the state government in 1807 when the legislature held its first session at the partially completed Statehouse. It was not the first capital but had followed Savannah, Augusta, and Louisville, for as settlers moved west, so did the legislators. Named for Governor John Milledge, it was a planned city, similar in design to Savannah. The downtown boasted of four public squares of 20 acres each, with the streets and squares surveyed in a checkerboard fashion. Each thoroughfare was 100 feet wide, except for Jefferson and Washington, boulevards that had parkways and were 20 feet wider. At the time of the Civil War, the four public squares held the state capitol, the railroad depot, the state prison, and the town cemetery.[1]

The city's social life varied according to the occupant of the governor's mansion. During Howell Cobb's two-year tenure as governor, which ended in 1853, life in the city had a festive air. A reception at the governor's mansion in 1851 revealed Cobb's lavish lifestyle. Oysters came by train from Savannah, and a 50-pound cake dominated the center of the dining room table, with a smaller cake at each end. Violins played, and to the delight of the visitors there was even a clarinet. Cobb enjoyed entertaining and loved to do it in grand style, liberally spending his wife's money.[2]

After graduation from the University of Georgia, Cobb had moved to the capital to begin his political life, boarding with a college friend, John B. Lamar. It was there that he had met Lamar's sister Mary Ann, a student at a local academy. She had inherited much of her father's vast estate, including some 200 slaves and thousands of acres in several counties. At the time of her marriage to Cobb in 1835, conservative estimates set her wealth at more than $100,000.[3]

She was never a strong woman, and the outbreak of the war intensified Mary Ann Cobb's anxieties. She suffered bouts of depression; over the years of her marriage she had worried about her husband's fidelity and even endured the embarrassment of having to sell some of her land to pay his mounting debts. At one point, Lamar family members took control of other lands to protect them from the consequences of Cobb's irresponsible behavior. With the war came more hardships; her brother John was killed during the Antietam campaign in 1862, and one of her younger children died not long afterward. She also worried about the safety of her husband and three oldest sons, all of whom served under Lee in Virginia. Cobb's return to Georgia in 1863 had alleviated some of her distress, but Sherman's departure from Atlanta had placed her husband, family, and possessions directly in harm's way. Hurricane, the plantation destroyed by Union soldiers, had been part of her inheritance.

State capitol at Milledgeville (*Harper's Weekly*)

Cobb had been followed in the governor's mansion by Herschel V. Johnson, who later served as a Confederate congressman. As Stephen A. Douglas's running mate in the 1860 presidential election, he was a well-known and widely respected political figure. In addition, he knew how to advance in important circles, for he had married a niece of a former president, James K. Polk. As governor, Johnson was considered a "scholarly man" and his wife a "lively intellect." The Johnsons' parties continued the lavish traditions set by the Cobbs.[4]

A stark contrast to Cobb and Johnson was Joseph E. Brown, the occupant of the governor's office on the day that Sherman's troops marched into the capital. Brown, a man from the north Georgia hills who was serving an unprecedented fourth term, also entertained, but he and his wife, Elizabeth, were religious and frugal. In keeping with their moderation, the first lady helped with the cooking and seldom served liquor to guests. Nevertheless, Milledgeville had retained its reputation for elegance. A Union prisoner who had passed through the town on a train bound for Andersonville in February 1864 noted: "This was a fine city, the public buildings were fine and costly. It was a very fashionable center for the high toned families of the Confederacy and the inhabitants were very aristocratic and wealthy."[5]

The rich and powerful, too, suffered the consequences of the war, however. Tragedy had struck the chief executive's mansion as a result of Sherman's invasion of Georgia: the governor's brother John, wounded in the fighting near Atlanta in late August, had been rushed to Milledgeville but soon died. As Sherman marched toward Atlanta, the ladies of Milledgeville had organized a hospital, and during the last days of August the hospital of the state militia had moved to the capital as well. As the fighting for Atlanta intensified, there were so many patients that the wounded had to be housed in tents. Refugees fleeing Sherman's path also flooded the city.

To protect the town, Brown had impressed 500 slaves to build fortifications, but as Sherman approached in late November, there were no soldiers in the newly constructed trenches. The state's adjutant and inspector general, Henry C. Wayne, had around 600 men, including some cadets from the Georgia Military Institute who had fled from their campus at Marietta and about 150 inmates from the state prison who promised to fight for the South in exchange for freedom. But he had transferred the command to the town of Gordon, leaving no one at the capital. As Sherman neared the seat of government, even the governor and legislators fled, though one Federal general later recalled that "the servants of Governor Brown and negroes of Milledgeville spoke of him as a 'mighty good man.'"[6]

On the afternoon of November 22, Sherman's troops marched through nearly deserted streets. With Union flags flying and the bands playing patriotic tunes, the soldiers passed the heart of Georgia's government. Only former slaves welcomed the invaders, as the town's residents hid behind locked doors. By the next day most of the left wing had arrived, and Milledgeville became a military camp, with officers expropriating lodging in the fine homes while the majority of the infantry camped in plantation fields across the river. The weather remained cold, and soldiers tore down fences and outbuildings for firewood. Still, there was little wanton destruction. Vandals did pour molasses into the pipes of the Episcopal church's organ, but the only houses burned in the vicinity were those of State Treasurer John Jones and the country homes of Judge Iverson Harris and Dr. William A. Jarrett. Harris, Sherman learned, had encouraged civilians to adopt a scorched-earth policy to prevent his men from finding food, and the general had given permission for retaliation. At Jarrett's plantation the overseer, Patrick Kane, was shot when he tried to defend the property; his was the only known death in the region.[7]

Although Sherman did not allow his men to despoil the town, the majority of civilians stayed inside for the duration of the occupation. Union soldiers enjoyed petty vandalism, most of which, even if not permanently harmful, disturbed and frightened local residents. Rowdy soldiers held a mock session of the legislature in the statehouse, disavowing the ordinance of secession and breaking furniture and windows in the process. "Some very humorous legislation was done by this transient body of law-makers," recalled a Union general. More seriously, some soldiers ransacked valuable government papers and books, tossing them into the statehouse yard. Fortunately, officials had previously removed the most important legislative documents to safety.[8]

As he had done in Atlanta, Sherman authorized the destruction of all military matériel. Soldiers dumped stores from the state magazine into the river and then blew up the structure—damaging two churches on the square in the process—and torched the nearby arsenal. The state penitentiary was also burned but not by Sherman; local residents admitted that the prison fire had been set by convicts left behind by General Wayne. Some cotton was destroyed, but most remained safe in warehouses, untouched by the Union troops. Several businesses—including a mill, a textile factory, and a foundry—escaped harm because their owners were not Georgians. Henry Hitchcock of the general's staff noted, "State House and Governor's Mansion all safe (glad of it) and people of the town say Yankees treated them much better than expected. Better than some of them deserved, I say." Sherman even "spared one man's cotton who has been engaged in running blockade from Georgia into Tennessee."[9]

In April 1865, Sherman told his wife in a short letter that he was forwarding by a soldier some items taken during the march. "I now send you a seal taken by some soldier off some public Document which I have no doubt was one of the Old Indian Treaties made by the Proprietors of the Colony of Georgia in the Old Colonial Times," he informed Ellen. "You can safely label this seal— Official Seal of the Colony of Georgia at the time of General Oglethorpe—taken at Milledgeville by a Soldier of Shermans Army November 1864."[10]

While the Union soldiers plundered and played, Milledgeville residents remained apprehensive. They not only worried about the troops but feared the growing numbers of slaves following the army. One Milledgeville slave, a boy named Allen Brantley, caught the eye of some sympathetic soldiers with his ability to manage unruly draft animals. As a result, they invited him to join the march, and after the war he produced enough evidence of his service with Sherman to obtain a pension.[11] This was not a typical circumstance, however.

Milledgeville meant little to Sherman; his goal was to reach the coast before his supplies ran out, so after two days the soldiers abandoned the state capital. Following on the heels of the infantry, Sherman's cavalry passed through the town before the residents could feel safe and assess the damage. Although major structures and residences had suffered little physical damage, there was not a fence or outbuilding left standing. Food was nonexistent, so survival was the immediate objective of Milledgeville residents, many of whom had lost all their winter stores. Fortunately for them, some Confederate cavalry captured about fifty head of cattle from the invaders and brought the herd back to the town. Mayor Boswell B. DeGraffenreid gladly accepted the peace offering (the Rebels, too, had taken food from the locals immediately after Sherman's passage). Even Howell Cobb tried to help, forwarding 5,000 rations of cornmeal and 18 head of cattle. A local paper reported, with some humor, that the mayor "acknowledged not only the corn but also the Cobb." Even a London merchant sent several thousand dollars in relief funds; in fact, he provided money for people all along Sherman's route.[12]

When the Union columns finally marched out of the capital, resident Anna Maria Green wrote, "This morning the last of the vandals left our city and burned the bridge after them—and leaving suffering and desolation behind them, and embittering every heart." Eliza Andrews, who passed through Milledgeville three weeks later, overheard a man say as she neared the town, "Milledgeville's like hell; you kin get thar easy enough, but gittin' out agin would beat the Devil himself."[13]

Realistically, the state capital suffered more from its geographical isolation than from anything Sherman did. Milledgeville had always been difficult to reach, and now both the Central of Georgia Railroad, which connected the town to the outside world, and the bridge over the Oconee River were out of commission. Wagons, carriages, and animals to pull them were scarce, making it difficult to travel anywhere. The town never recovered its prewar political prominence, for in 1868 the state constitutional convention voted to relocate the seat of government to Atlanta, a much more accessible location. Atlanta, which had grown steadily after Sherman's visit, had by then almost ten times more people than Milledgeville's approximately 2,300. Brigadier General William P. Carlin wrote in his memoirs that "Milledgeville seemed to be a sleepy and quiet old place," and Georgians "had the good sense since the war to remove [the state's] seat of Government to Atlanta, an energetic and enterprising city."[14] Georgia was the only state to relocate its capital partly as a result of the war. Although some Union soldiers remembered Milledgeville as quaint, one man had written his brother, "We passed through the Capital of the state, it is a miserable one Horse city not worthy [of] the name of city."[15]

The seat of government fared better than Griswoldville, a small factory town nine miles east of Macon, directly in the path of Sherman's right wing. On the same day that Sherman's left wing marched into Milledgeville, soldiers from the right wing clashed with Confederates there.

Founded in 1849 by Connecticut-born Samuel Griswold, the Jones County village was a stop on the Central of Georgia Railroad. A visitor in 1852 had even noted that it was the "prettiest town" on the route. The streets were "wide and straight and planted with trees . . . and it promises to become a flourishing place." The town had grown so rapidly that by 1861 it was second only to Clinton, the county seat, which numbered around 300 residents.[16]

When the war came, Griswold adapted his cotton gin factory to meet the needs of the Confederacy. The governor's call for military arms encouraged him to switch his production to weapons, and by mid-1862, twenty-two machines were producing a six-shooter percussion-cap pistol—patterned on the .36-caliber Colt Navy revolver—which sold for $40.00. The *Macon Telegraph* reported: "This is a strong illustration of the power of the South to supply her own wants. We certainly had no idea that a manufactory of Colt's pistols would spring up near Macon in 1862." More than 800 pikes, all stamped "S. Griswold," were shipped to the armory at the state capital in the spring of 1862. The small industrial town also served as a training center for troops and as the location of a hospital.[17] When Jefferson Davis had visited briefly in October 1863, a newspaper noted that even though slaves made up most of the labor force, they seemed to take pride in their work. Upon Davis's arrival "about forty Negroes, laborers in Mr. Griswold's pistol shops at that place, had collected and manifested great anxiety to see Mr. Davis. Being told of it, he got off the car and went the rounds, taking each one by the hand and giving him a pleasant word."[18]

All the industries of central Georgia naturally attracted Union attention, though the main targets were weapon-producing facilities, although Camp Ogelthorpe, a small prison on Macon's southern perimeter, had also drawn notice. The Confederacy had about 1,400 officers confined at this stockade at Macon, and in July 1864, Major General George Stoneman had determined to free the captives. With any luck he also intended to liberate the prisoners of war in Camp Sumter at Andersonville. Stoneman's path took him through Clinton, where his cavalrymen reportedly "entered private houses and stripped ladies of rings and pins; broke open drawers and trunks, stole silver and plate of every description." At one residence, troopers told the mistress "to deal out wine in the wine cellar." Doubtless the raiders enjoyed frightening the local residents; they even threatened to hang an elderly man north of the town of Hillsboro for firing on the raiding party. Local newspapers reported various atrocities, for cavalry, operating independently, frequently committed numerous, and unreported, offenses. Stoneman, however, was captured after a one-sided battle at Sunshine Church near Macon at the end of July. Although exchanged by the time Sherman marched through Georgia, Stoneman did not return to the lower South; the Confederates faced Judson Kilpatrick instead.[19]

From the beginning of the campaign, Confederate cavalry under Joe Wheeler skirmished with Union cavalry under Kilpatrick. As the Union horsemen moved south, they rode unopposed into

Clinton on November 19. One infantryman later described the town: "The situation of Clinton is that of calm, quiet, peaceful solitude, embowered by trees, which add by their shade a degree of beauty and repose to the scene," he wrote. "The country round it presents a very fine aspect, being well cultivated and ornamented. A little hill, standing to the westward of the town, commands a view of a rich and cultivated valley."[20]

Wheeler, spreading his horsemen thin, had little success in stopping the enemy cavalry's path of destruction. Union soldiers burned Sunshine Church; the town of Irwinton had its "principal buildings" put to the torch; and structures in Hillsboro were wrecked. Clinton suffered as well, since the extreme cold weather meant that Union soldiers continued to use anything available to build fires for warmth. One-third of the small town disappeared. Foragers also scoured the countryside. A Clinton resident later reported, "All through our streets and commons are to be seen dead horses and mules—entrails of hogs and cattle killed, and in many instances, the hams only taken—oxen carts even taken away so that we are not able to remove this offensive matter." At Griswoldville, horsemen burned the factories, mills, gun works, and railroad depot. Troopers torched most of the houses as well, except Griswold's home, which Kilpatrick used as his headquarters.[21]

Confederate leaders in Macon, isolated because Union horsemen had cut the telegraph lines, waited for word from Wheeler. Richard Taylor, who had hurried to join the state's defenders, arrived in the city in the "bitterest" weather he recalled in the lower South. Other leaders assembling in Macon were Howell Cobb, Governor Brown, Robert Toombs, and Gustavus W. Smith, commander of the Georgia Militia and other state troops. President Davis had telegraphed Cobb "to get out every man who can render any service" in the army "even for a short period." Davis encouraged the use of slaves to block the roads and even suggested using "shells prepared to explode by pressure." Hardee, who had gone to Savannah before General Taylor's arrival, concluded that Sherman's true objective was not Macon but Augusta, the site of some of the Confederacy's most valuable munitions works: powder factories that provided ammunition to Lee's army. Consequently, Davis had dispatched Braxton Bragg to Augusta to prepare a defense. Hardee, believing that no competent military commander would forgo an opportunity to raze such an important facility, ordered units from around Macon to leave for Augusta as well. The force of around

1,900 men was a mixture of soldiers from the Georgia State Line
and Georgia militia, accompanied by the Fourteenth Georgia Light
Artillery, all under the command of Pleasant J. Philips.[22]

While the Confederates worried about which town to protect,
the Union commanders continued to fret about the safety of the
supply trains. General Howard detailed part of the Fifteenth Corps
to provide cover for the wagons, since he had heard that Wheeler
was still in the area. Unknown to him, however, Wheeler had moved
east to harass Sherman's left wing as it advanced out of Milledgeville. In fact, conditions across central Georgia were confusing for
both sides. As Philips neared Griswoldville, he was joined by some
400 men of Major F. W. C. Cook's Reserve battalions. Philips, thinking there were few enemy troops in the area, moved his enlarged
command along the rail lines. One mile east of Griswoldville the
Confederates encountered some Union skirmishers, and Philips,
who believed he outnumbered the enemy, boldly went on the attack. He had instructions to avoid an engagement, but he was not a
professional soldier, and it was later said he had enjoyed too much
whiskey.

To protect the Union supply wagons, Brigadier General
Charles C. Walcutt had moved six infantry regiments to a ridge
east of Griswoldville, deploying his men behind a barricade of fence
rails. Philips, not realizing he had encountered experienced infantrymen, unwisely ordered a frontal assault on Walcutt's line. As
the Rebels advanced across an open field, the Union veterans, many
armed with efficient repeating rifles, took aim, fired, and watched
men writhe and fall as the bullets hit their mark. Captain Charles
Wills of the 103d Illinois reported, "It was awful the way we slaughtered those men." After the battle, Northern soldiers were distressed
to discover that their opponents were not regular Confederates but
mainly old men and boys from the Georgia militia, some not even
fifteen years old. A soldier who walked across the battlefield the
next day recalled, "Some one was groaning. We moved a few bodies, and there was a boy with a broken arm and leg—just a boy of
14-years-old; and beside him, cold in death, lay his Father, two
Brothers, and an Uncle." Another Union veteran concluded, "I hope
we will never have to shoot at such men again." A Georgia militiaman wrote home that after the battle the doctors were busy cutting
off arms and legs. "They was wounded in all possible manner that
you can imagine," he noted. "It was the distressingest time I ever
saw in my life."[23]

The fight at Griswoldville was barely more than a skirmish, and the loss on the Union side was relatively light: thirteen Union soldiers died, and seventy-nine were wounded. The Rebels, however, counted fifty-one killed and 472 wounded. A Confederate soldier told his wife that the battle "ceased about night, when we withdrew, leaving some of our killed and wounded on the field exposed to the severities of a very cold night. . . . Oh, that this cruel war could stop! I desire very much to live at home in peace with you and the dear children." Yet as Georgia families mourned the dead and tended the wounded, Northerners celebrated: Thursday, November 24, was Lincoln's official day of Thanksgiving.[24]

Griswoldville would be one of those events that ensured a place for Sherman's name in the history books. Nothing much of the town survived. It was primarily a factory town; those factories had turned to war production; as a result, Union soldiers destroyed almost everything except Griswold's home. After Griswold died in 1867 the town all but disappeared, adding to the folklore surrounding Sherman's march through Georgia.

Milledgeville had fared better, but when Brown returned to the governor's mansion, he found almost everything gone. This was not the result of Sherman's passage—the soldiers had no way to cart off heavy furniture—but instead the work of civilians who appropriated items of all description during the confusion that followed the brief Union occupation. The governor threatened to search and seize the property from private homes but apparently decided instead to worry about the survival of his family. (In spite of her north Georgia roots, Elizabeth Brown knew little about farming. She told her mother that she could not understand why the eggs did not hatch—a more experienced farm wife would have known it was because of the lack of a rooster.) Still, there was nothing left to do but give thanks that Sherman had left, and wait to see where he would move next.[25]

NOTES

1. James C. Bonner, *Milledgeville: Georgia's Antebellum Capital* (Macon: Mercer University Press, 1978), 17.
2. Ibid., 143.
3. Ibid., 141.
4. Ibid., 145–48.

5. Private Robert Knox Sneden, a Canadian-born New Yorker, noted that Milledgeville was at the head of the Savannah River (*Eye of the Storm*, 202). He was incorrect; it is the Oconee River.

6. Carlin, *Memoirs*, 151.

7. Bonner, *Milledgeville*, 187.

8. Carlin, *Memoirs*, 152.

9. Hitchcock, *Letters and Campaign Diaries*, 94–95.

10. Sherman, *Sherman's Civil War*, 850.

11. Bonner, *Milledgeville*, 192. According to Bonner, Brantley used this money to set himself up financially and even to send his grandchildren to college.

12. Bonner, *Milledgeville*, 193; *Macon Telegraph*, December 3, 1864; *Milledgeville Southern Recorder*, January 3, 1865.

13. Anna Maria Green in *The Journal of a Milledgeville Girl, 1861–1867*, ed. James C. Bonner (Athens: University of Georgia Press, 1964), 63; Eliza Frances Andrews, *The War-time Journal of a Georgia Girl, 1864–1865* (1908; reprint, Lincoln: University of Nebraska Press, 1997), 28.

14. In the 1870 census, Atlanta had 21,289 inhabitants and Milledgeville 2,313, with 51 percent of those black. Of the state capitals in the former Confederacy, only Tallahassee had fewer people (although only four of those former capitals had achieved populations over 10,000). Bonner, *Milledgeville*, 232. See also Carlin, *Memoirs*, 151.

15. John Gourlie to "Dear Brother," December 19, 1864, Civil War Misc. Collection, United States Army Military History Institute, Carlisle Barracks, Pennsylvania (hereafter cited as USAMHI).

16. Most of the background information about this town comes from William Harris Bragg, *Griswoldville* (Macon: Mercer University Press, 2000), 10, 12, 15.

17. *Macon Telegraph*, August 5, 1862; Bragg, *Griswoldville*, 19–20. Arvin Nye Gunnison, originally from New Hampshire, was Griswold's partner.

18. *Macon Telegraph*, November 2, 1863.

19. *Augusta Chronicle and Sentinel*, August 5, 1864; *Macon Telegraph*, August 4, 1864. John McKissick was taken away by Union horsemen after "he took his shotgun and blew one of the Yankees out of the saddle," but later he returned home safely. Bragg, *Griswoldville*, 39, 77.

20. George W. Pepper, *Personal Recollections of Sherman's Campaigns in Georgia and the Carolinas* (Zanesville, OH: O. H. Dunne, 1866), 241.

21. Bragg, *Griswoldville*, 99; *Macon Telegraph*, November 29, 1864.

22. Richard Taylor, *Destruction and Reconstruction: Personal Experiences of the Late War in the United States* (Edinburgh: William Blackwood & Sons, 1879), 280–81; *O.R.* 44, 865. For an explanation of the various state units, see William Harris Bragg, *Joe Brown's Army: The Georgia State Line, 1862–1865* (Macon, GA: Mercer University Press, 1987).

23. Wills, *Army Life*, 323–24; Upson, *With Sherman to the Sea*, 138; Jonathan Bridges, *Letters of Jonathan Bridges: A Confederate Soldier of Stewart County, Georgia*, comp. Richard M. Patchin and Deborah Jean Patchin (N.p., n.d.), 58; Jefferson Davis to Howell Cobb, November 16, 1864, Howell Cobb Papers, Hargrett Library, University of Georgia, Athens.

24. Lane, "*Dear Mother*," 335–36.

25. Bonner, *Milledgeville*, 197.

CHAPTER SIX

"WE HEAR OF TERRIBLE TIMES BELOW"
Southeast Georgia

AS THE UNION COLUMNS moved south, both terrain and weather improved. The rain stopped; the temperature rose; and drying road-beds allowed the wagons to roll along without the need for sol-diers to lay logs for traction. As pine trees, some 30 to 60 feet high, replaced the fertile fields of central Georgia and pine needles cov-ered the roads, food for the men and fodder for the animals be-came harder to find. Soldiers were also growing "anxious to get where [they would] have some other fuel" since the smoke from pine wood was becoming too "disagreeable."[1]

The land became sandier and flatter, and cypress swamps, their waters covered with algae, appeared alongside the roadways. Sherman's columns crossed the fall line, the geological break run-ning across the state south of which the area had once been cov-ered by the ocean; there red clay changed to the sand of the ancient seabed. As a result, there were fewer farms and foraging parties increased their looting and unauthorized scavenging. One local resident recalled that "4 or 5 yankees came, professing they would behave as gentlemen. These gentlemen, however stole my gold watch, and silver spoons, besides whiskey, tobacco, and a hat or two apiece." Later that day, the man added, "4 more came, and got a few hats, and one fiddle, and some whiskey." That evening two more arrived "and got some whiskey, a few hats, etc." Sometimes Southerners retaliated; one report claimed that at least sixty-four Union soldiers had been executed by either the Confederate cav-alry or local residents. Some corpses were reported to have had their throats slit, and their bodies, left for the army to find, carried signs such as "Death to all foragers." But resistance was rare, for the Federals penalized such actions by burning barns and fences and, in extreme cases, even the houses.[2]

Upon leaving Milledgeville, Sherman's left wing turned toward Sandersville. Before the main columns arrived, Wheeler's cavalry attacked some Union horsemen, and captured several men, who were later executed by Confederate vigilantes. As Sherman approached the town, the residents expected retribution for the deaths; Major Hitchcock on Sherman's staff believed that the general "would be justified by the laws of war in destroying the whole town" for the murders. But Sherman decided instead to burn only the courthouse and business district, leaving private homes intact. Also, just to the south, at Tennille, Federals burned the warehouses and the depot, and destroyed water tanks. Moreover, Sherman turned a blind eye to pillaging and looting, feeling that such punishment should follow when Southerners resisted.[3]

From Sandersville the left wing moved for Louisville, Georgia's previous state capital. When the Federals arrived, a fire broke out and, before it could be contained, burned several homes. Unruly soldiers pillaged and ransacked residences, and a second fire consumed many of the remaining structures. Rumors of widespread destruction spread across the state, and Minerva McClatchey at Marietta wrote in her diary on December 1: "Everything is uncertain, we hear of terrible times below—where Sherman is marching. They are very hard on refugees."[4]

The actual physical damage left in the wake of Sherman's army is impossible to calculate. One problem is the absence of evidence, particularly concerning attacks on women; in his memoirs Sherman insisted that he "never heard of any cases of murder or rape." One documented assault did occur in Midway, a small community south of Milledgeville. Kate Latimer Nichols, the 27-year-old wife of Captain James H. Nichols of the Governor's Horse Guards, was bedridden when two Union soldiers entered her home; her husband was away fighting in Virginia. A Milledgeville resident wrote in her diary, "The worst of their acts was committed to poor Mrs. Nichols—violence done, and atrocity committed that ought to make her husband an enemy unto death. Poor woman I fear she has been driven crazy." The Savannah paper reported on December 6 that "the incarnate devils ravished some of the nicest ladies in Milledgeville. One of their unfortunate victims was, we learn, consigned to the Asylum on Monday."[5]

No female felt safe. Black women, too, suffered at the hands of Union soldiers; many Northerners contrasted them favorably, "particularly good looking ones, decked in satins and silks," with backwoods white women. A letter written from Clinton on November 26 claimed that "female servants were taken and villified without mercy, by their officers; and in some instances when they were reared as tenderly as whites." One former slave was later quoted as recalling "a heap of talk 'bout de scandlous way dem Yankee sojers been treatin' Negro 'omans and gals." On one plantation, black men put the women in a house and staked a guard.[6]

Color made no difference in looting, either; Union soldiers often confiscated property belonging to free blacks just as quickly as that of white inhabitants. Mary Ross Bellamy, a free woman of color who lived near Milledgeville, initially celebrated the arrival of Union liberators, only to find that despite her protests the soldiers emptied her barns and fields and took her horse and hogs.[7]

Whatever violence there actually was against women did not go altogether unnoticed by Union authorities. John Bass, a 16-year-old Illinois private, was court-martialed for attempted rape, although the evidence was weak and even the lady in question admitted that Bass had never touched her. Rather, she claimed, he had pulled a revolver after she called him a "Nigger Stealer." Still, the court found the young man guilty; his head was shaved, and he was dishonorably discharged. Bass's commanding officer complained, but General Howard pointed out that "he must make an example of some one and just as well a 48th [Illinois] man as anyone else."[8]

The Richmond government could do nothing to halt Sherman's progress, and Georgians were left to their own resources. In the wake of the army's advance, a woman had observed, "This ended the passing of Shermans army by my place leaving me poorer by thirty thousand dollars than I was yesterday morning. And a much stronger rebel." Realizing the impact of Sherman's march, she added, "Oh the horrors the horrors of war." Another Georgian complained to her cousin that the government had done nothing to prevent the march: "I never could understand the policy of Hood's going off to Tennessee and leaving the Yankees in our midst to make their way undisputed to our seaport cities. We feel the deepest anxiety, and know not what to expect."[9]

Tension filled the air. A Georgia militiaman stationed near Savannah wrote his wife in Stewart County on December 6: "I have not heard one word from you in seven weeks and I am very uneasy about you all. I never was so frightened about any thing in my life." On the fourteenth, he told her, "The Yankees are all around us nearly."[10]

Why did Sherman spare the city of Augusta? In his memoirs, he stated that destroying the Augusta Powder Works was not necessary; he intended to tear up the railroad carrying goods to Virginia when he moved into South Carolina. But this excuse was written long after the war, for in November 1864, Sherman did not know that he would receive permission for a march into South Carolina. Once he reached Savannah, he would find that Lincoln wanted his army transferred to Virginia by water, and he would again have to convince Washington of the value of a march through Rebel territory. So there must have been other reasons.

Each county has its legend explaining why Sherman did not destroy various towns, but the one for Augusta is perhaps the best known. As the story goes, Sherman spared the city because of his affection for Cecelia Stovall, a Georgia beauty he may have met when he was stationed in the South in the 1840s. Family lore tells that during his fight for Atlanta, Sherman spared her plantation home in Cass County (although she had already fled) and sent her a note by a slave: "My Dear Madam: You once said that you pitied the man who ever became my foe. My answer was that I would shield and protect you. That I have done. Forgive all else; I am but a soldier. W. T. Sherman."[11] It is possible that Cecelia, who had married Charles Shelman, was with her brother's family in Augusta as Sherman's columns passed, but Union soldiers had a more practical, and possibly more accurate, explanation. They believed that Augusta had received reinforcements, for there were rumors that either Joseph E. Johnston or James Longstreet was there. "Sherman don't know what is at Augusta," observed a major, "neither do we know. A rebel army of 50,000 men may be on us before daylight tomorrow."[12]

After the war, Sherman was well aware of the questions surrounding Augusta. He wrote the Georgia journalist Pleasant Stovall almost a quarter-century later that though it was true he had been in the city as a lieutenant of the Third Artillery in 1844, there was no connection between that visit and his wartime activities. "If the people of Augusta think I slighted them in the winter of 1864–65 by reason of personal friendships formed in 1844, they are mistaken; or if they think I made a mistake in strategy, let them say so." Writing from New York City in 1888, he sarcastically told Stovall, while lecturing him about the South's folly in fighting the North, that "with the President's consent I think I can send a detachment of a hundred thousand or so of Sherman's Bummers and their descendants who will finish up the job without charging Uncle Sam a cent."[13]

As the left wing—for whatever reason—skirted Augusta, the right wing bypassed the Confederate prison at Andersonville. Since, at Hood's request, Richmond authorities had removed the prisoners to the newly constructed Camp Lawton outside Millen, the notorious compound was nearly empty and no longer interested Sherman. It was not in his path—but Millen was. The sleepy little town lay on the railroad between Augusta and Savannah, and the presence of a spring with clear water nearby had made it suitable for the site of a prisoner-of-war camp to accommodate the overflow from Andersonville. Designed to hold 40,000, Camp Lawton had been hastily built in September 1864 by 300 prisoners and 500 slaves. The 40-acre stockade, guarded by three forts, received its first prisoners in October, soon after Hood requested that Andersonville be emptied. By November more than 10,000 were in residence.

Stockade at Camp Lawton (*Leslie's Illustrated*)

The cold weather that had plagued Sherman's march had also made life miserable for the prisoners at Camp Lawton. On November 11 a Federal soldier had written, "Ice formed on the edges of the brook and many of the prisoners had to walk about camp all night to keep from freezing." On the seventeenth, he observed, "Cold weather and snow. Three of our men were frozen to death last night in the stockade! Large fires are going, but many are so reduced in vitality that they easily froze notwithstanding." And the following day, "There fell about two inches of snow last night, and today we have cold winds, which must make the poor fellows in the stockade suffer terribly." On another note, he added, "The excitement continues, and Sherman's moving this way hurries up matters with the Rebels who look rather scared, and want to get away anywhere."[14]

Richmond quickly ordered the prisoners transferred, and early in the morning of November 20, Rebel guards prodded them onto open railroad flatcars. The captives suffered intensely from the cold weather as the cars headed for Savannah. When the last man left the camp, recalled a Federal soldier, "large clouds of black smoke in the woods on both sides of the track showed where storehouses and bales of cotton were being burnt to prevent them falling into 'Yankee hands.' " The prisoners were transferred to temporary locations in towns such as Blackshear and Thomasville, although many ended up back in Andersonville after Sherman left the state.[15]

For Georgians, the situation had become critical. As the last prison trains arrived at Millen to pick up inmates, they were "switched off for two hours to allow continuous trains to pass, loaded with household furniture, cotton, women and children, and lots of Negro slaves," fleeing from Sherman's troops. Governor Brown had asked Richmond for help as soon as the Union columns left Atlanta, and the secretary of war had assured Brown that the government would do all it could with its "limited resources" but added that any assistance would come only "in consistency with general safety"—meaning that Virginia still came first in military thinking.[16]

President Davis telegraphed Robert E. Lee for advice. "Please give me your views as to the action proper under the circumstances of Sherman's movement," he wrote. His concern was so great that he asked if Lee could come to Richmond to discuss the matter in person. One topic he wanted to address was the possibility of sending reinforcements to Georgia from the Virginia theater. Almost every time that suggestion was made (with the exception of Longstreet's trip to Georgia in the late summer of 1863), Lee had convinced Davis of the imprudence of such a move. Clearly, though, Beauregard needed help if he hoped to stop Sherman, and the evidence suggests that Davis agreed with Beauregard but was unable to persuade Lee to release any men. Not long after conferring with

Lee, Davis told Hardee at Savannah: "Beyond the force sent some time since to Augusta, General Lee has not thus far found himself able to detach troops from his command. Should a change of circumstances permit further aid to be sent, no time will be lost."[17]

Union soldiers visiting a plantation (*Leslie's Illustrated*)

As the left wing headed in the direction of Millen, the right wing passed through Irwinton on its journey south. Local citizens had buried "a great many things to keep them from the 'vandals,' " wrote a soldier, "and the boys soon found it out. Hundreds of them were armed with sharpened sticks probing the earth 'prospecting.' They found a little of everything, and I guess they took it all [from] the owners, eatables and drinkables." As a result of this behavior the soldiers had the order prohibiting pillaging "read to us for I guess the 20th time." Beyond Irwinton the troops passed through three miles of "miserable pine swamps" before crossing the Oconee River at Ball's Ferry. An Illinois soldier said it took ten boats to hold the pontoon bridge, but he estimated the river to be only 8 steps wide. Near Riddleville some Northern soldiers marveled at their first Southern magnolia, and farther to the southeast, Union troops came upon the home of a German who declared that "he had been ordered to join the army one, two, three, twenty times, but had told them that he would rather be shot than take up arms against the U.S." The Twelfth Indiana band honored him with a serenade as it passed.[18]

Once President Davis recognized that Sherman's march through Georgia could not be stopped, he knew that the only relief lay in Hood's defeating Union forces in Tennessee. On Wednesday, November 30, when Sherman's march was two weeks old and there was still no news of the Confederate army, Davis told Beauregard, "Until Hood reaches the country proper of the enemy, he can scarcely change the plans for Sherman's or Grant's campaigns. They would, I think, regard the occupation of Tennessee and Kentucky as of minor importance." That same day an official in Richmond recorded in his diary, "It is reported that Gen. Hood is still marching North, and is near Nashville." An Ohio soldier made an accurate assessment when he wrote, "Sherman and Hood here both playing 'smash' Hood has come one way and Sherman gone the other. Neither one having any line for supplies of rations or ammunition. But Hood cannot take any important place here and Sherman can go just where he pleases." Hopes that Sherman might reverse his direction and return north to fight Hood rapidly faded.[19]

Eliza Andrews, who crossed the region east of the Oconee River after the army's passage, wrote that in the "Burnt Country" nothing remained but isolated houses. "The fields were trampled down and the road was lined with carcasses of horses, hogs, and cattle. . . . The stench in some places was unbearable, every few hundred yards we had to hold our noses or stop them with cologne." Scattered Confederate soldiers ate "raw turnips, meat skins, parched corn—anything they could find, even picking up the loose grain that Sherman's horses had left." Before taking the ferry over the river at Milledgeville, Andrews saw the fields where enemy soldiers had camped, and the "carcasses of slaughtered animals . . . raised a horrible stench."[20]

The chaos in the countryside encouraged depredations by escaped slaves, deserters from both armies, and even Confederate cavalrymen—who actually caused the most complaints. Wheeler's force never exceeded 3,500 men, and he seldom had more than 2,000 under his immediate command. His orders were to drive off the horses and mules on farms and plantations in advance of the enemy columns to prevent Sherman from capturing or killing the animals. He also had orders to "subsist upon the country." Wheeler pointed out that his men were living on "bread baked upon boards and stones and meat boiled upon sticks." Furthermore, the troopers had not been paid in twelve months and had received no allowances for clothing. Yet to some Georgians, Confederates foraging for food seemed no different from Northerners doing the same; indeed, some Yankee infantry displayed extremely good manners as they emptied barns and corncribs—courtesy not always extended by the Rebel horsemen.[21]

Despite such grievances, Wheeler's troopers provided the only real defense that Georgians had during Sherman's advance. After it appeared that Sherman had no designs on Macon, Wheeler had crossed the Oconee River and, hearing that Kilpatrick was moving toward Augusta, headed east. Early on November 27 the Rebel cavalry attacked Kilpatrick's camp, taking prisoners, flags, and horses. Kilpatrick was said to have been in the company of a lady at a house nearby and "very nearly captured." Without doubt, much of the damage in this region came from cavalrymen burning corncribs, cotton gins, barns, and houses. Unlike the infantry, which was under more strict control, the horsemen laid the land to waste. Northern troopers set the town of Waynesboro on fire, but Wheeler's men arrived just as the enemy fled and managed to extinguish the flames. Fighting continued into the following day, with some 1,800 Rebels chasing about 3,700 Union horsemen, but ended when Kilpatrick withdrew to the safety of the infantry camps. "Confound the cavalry," wrote an officer when he learned of the fiasco. "They're good for nothing but to run down horses and steal chickens. I'd rather have one good regiment of infantry than the whole of Kilpatrick's cavalry."[22]

Not only was Wheeler at a numerical disadvantage, but his men were tired. For the previous five months the Rebel horsemen had been on the move, often averaging 16 miles a day. Details searched for rations, annoying local citizenry, but it was frequently "midnight before supper could be prepared," and the men had to "be in the saddle before daylight." But it was not until the fighting near Waynesboro that the Federal superiority in strength finally began to show. "This has been a regular field day, and we have had 'lots of fun' chasing Wheeler and his cavalry," wrote a Union officer about the fighting near Buckhead Church on December 4. "Kilpatrick is full of fun and frolic and he was in excellent spirits all day, for Wheeler and he were classmates at West Point, and he was elated at the idea of whipping his classmate." Being part of a cavalry fight would be "just about as much fun as a fox hunt," he added, if not for the fact that men were being "hurt all the time."[23]

On a more serious note, Kilpatrick told Sherman that some of his troopers had been killed after being taken prisoner, and he wanted permission to strike back. Sherman, aware that if he allowed unchecked retaliation, the fighting might escalate into a true guerrilla war of the kind going on in Kansas and Missouri, cautioned his impulsive cavalry chief to be "very careful" in regard to punishment; Kilpatrick could, however, inform Wheeler that any further murders would not go unpunished. "When our men are found and you are fully convinced the enemy have killed them after surrender in fair battle, or have mutilated their bodies after having been killed in fair battle," Sherman stated, "you may hang and mutilate man for man without regard to rank."[24]

While Kilpatrick's feint toward Augusta was occupying the Rebel cavalry, Sherman contemplated his next step. He had heard rumors that Braxton Bragg had 10,000 soldiers in Augusta who might march on the Union columns at any moment, but that information did not seem to trouble the general. He told Slocum that if they could draw Bragg toward Savannah, they could "turn on him and send him off at a tangent." Sherman had obtained a Savannah paper on December 2, and he knew that the Rebels had scattered their forces among Macon, Augusta, and Savannah. His soldiers were less confident, for this was the first time the Rebels had allowed them to advance relatively unopposed in over three years of war.[25]

Union commanders in South Carolina, though they could not pinpoint Sherman's whereabouts, wanted to help. They knew that Confederates threatened the Federal columns on the north side of the Savannah River above the city. In an attempt to disperse the Rebels, Brigadier General John P. Hatch advanced on the Charleston & Savannah Railroad, the supply line for the defenders in the Georgia port.[26] The Confederate response came quickly. Colonel Charles J. Colcock had barely 400 available men, and many were stationed at key points along the tracks so Major John Jenkins, Jones's second in command, called for reinforcements from Charleston and Savannah. One of those Georgians to respond was Gustavus Smith, whose troops had just fought at Griswoldville. In an unusual move, the Georgia militiamen agreed to cross the state line, and the battle came on November 30 at Honey Hill, not far from Grahamville, a South Carolina summer resort.

For a small battle, there was immense slaughter. Yet this time it was Union soldiers whose bodies covered the ground after several futile assaults through a swampy expanse covered with trees and brush. "We fought in a forest dense and marshy," remembered Sergeant James M. Trotter of the Fifty-fifth Massachusetts (Colored), "and it was almost impossible on this account to maneuver more than half our troops." Captain William D. Crane of the Fifty-fifth, who attempted to rally the soldiers by yelling that the enemy was only Georgia militia, was killed by an artillery shell. After the fighting ended, a Southerner claimed that outside the Rebel earthworks he saw "some sixty or seventy bodies in a space of about an acre, many of which were horribly mutilated by shells, some with half their heads shot off, and others completely disemboweled." Rows of black troops "lay five deep as dead as a mackeral." When Smith later reported his victory, he wrote that the "flight of the enemy during the night and the number of their dead left upon the field is evidence of the nature of the attacks as well as the defense."[27]

For the Federals, it was Griswoldville in reverse: 750 soldiers were dead or wounded, 138 were from the Twenty-fifth Ohio. Most of the casualties were from the black units in the battle: the Fifty-fourth and Fifty-fifth Massachusetts (Colored), and the Twenty-sixth, Thirty-second, Thirty-fourth, Thirty-fifth, and 102d U.S. Colored Troops. This was the first battle for the men of the Thirty-second and 102d, which lost sixty-four and twenty-three men, respectively.[28]

The Confederates had clearly won a decisive victory. But for the people of Savannah, the fighting at Honey Hill, only a short distance north of the Savannah River, was too close for comfort. Coupled with recent newspaper warnings of Sherman's advance, anxiety rose among local residents. Yet even as rumors spread, the editor of the *Savannah Republican* reassured his readers: "We are much inclined though, to regard this present movement simply as a raid, which will do its appointed damage and then come to grief. If it be really an expedition, on grand scale, for the cities of the coast, as represented elsewhere in our accounts from Yankee papers, then let them come here if they can." Since Hardee had made preparations for an attack, the editor tried to raise spirits among his readers by adding that the enemy would "find it a hard road to travel, if the people and the army but do their duty." Still, the people were "considerably excited, owing to various reports of the advance of the enemy."[29]

When the local paper finally declared that Augusta was Sherman's target, the panic subsided in Savannah. The mayor beseeched the people "to prepare & not flee," but reports changed hourly, and within a few days it became obvious that Sherman was headed for the southeast coast. It appeared that either Savannah or Charleston was his objective. As a result, on November 28, Mayor Richard Arnold called for all able-bodied men to report for duty.[30] To add to the tension, the paper printed a letter written from Atlanta under the heading "Atlanta as Left by Sherman: A City in Ruin." The article also estimated the Union strength (too low by many thousands) at 47,000 men and 130 guns. Even in the face of growing reality, most Savannah residents still felt that the general intended to go elsewhere. The newspaper's editor noted that he saw "little advantage in taking Savannah." Surely the "vandal chief" would go to Beaufort or Charleston instead.[31]

By December 4, however, it became clear that the Union army was headed for the Georgia coast. Letters appeared in the paper describing the destruction at Clinton and Milledgeville, and Confederate authorities appealed to civilians to aid the soldiers in the trenches outside the river port. As the weather turned colder, the soldiers manning the earthworks needed shoes and warm clothing, but many residents had already fled and could offer no help. James A. Williams ran an advertisement offering his "Valuable Plantation and Negroes for Sale"—he had retreated to East Florida. Nonetheless, the Masons of the Clinton Lodge held their December meeting at the Masonic Hall at the corner of Bull Street and Broughton.[32]

When it finally became obvious to the people of Savannah that they could no longer ignore Sherman, Mayor Arnold pleaded for "all men of every age, not absolutely incapacitated from disease" to come forward. Older men could man the fortifications; the younger ones could "act in the field." Realizing at last that the city's future was in jeopardy, he added, "No time is to be lost." Sherman was on his way.[33]

NOTES

1. *Reminiscences of the Civil War from Diaries of Members of the 103d Illinois Volunteer Infantry*, 156.
2. Lawrence Huff, " 'A Bitter Draught We have Had to Quaff': Sherman's March through the Eyes of Joseph Addison Turner," *Georgia Historical Quarterly* 72 (Summer 1988): 320; Glatthaar, *March to the Sea*, 128.

3. Hitchcock, *Marching with Sherman*, 98.

4. Minerva McClatchey, "A Brief Journal of a Part of the Year 1864," *Georgia Historical Quarterly* 51 (June 1967): 197–216.

5. Sherman, *Memoirs*, 2:183; Green, *Journal of a Milledgeville Girl*, 63. The *Savannah Daily Morning News* had taken the story from the *Augusta Register*. Green later tried to obliterate Mrs. Nichols's name in her diary. Whatever actually happened to Mrs. Nichols will never be known, but it was widely believed locally that she had been raped.

6. *Savannah Daily Morning News*, December 2, 1864, quoting a letter in the *Macon Telegraph*; Paul D. Escott, "The Context of Freedom: Georgia's Slaves during the Civil War," *Georgia Historical Quarterly* 58 (Spring 1974): 93.

7. Adele Logan Alexander, *Ambiguous Lives: Free Women of Color in Rural Georgia, 1789–1879* (Fayetteville: University of Arkansas Press, 1991), 134–38.

8. Glatthaar, *March to the Sea*, 73.

9. Burge, *Diary*, 163, 165; Myers, *Children of Pride*, 1216.

10. Bridges, *Letters*, 62, 64.

11. Cecelia's brother, Marcellus A. Stovall, had left West Point before graduating; he joined the Confederate army and became a brigadier general in 1863. He lived in Rome, in northwest Georgia, but it seems likely that he had moved his family to Augusta when Rome became unsafe. Lucy Josephine Cunyus, *The History of Bartow County* ([Cartersville, GA]: Tribune Publishing Co., 1933), 250–51. Although the story of Cecelia (also spelled Cecilia) comes from Cunyus, it was confirmed by a family historian. C. L. Bragg to the author, August 29 and September 15, 1998. After the war, Pleasant A. Stovall (then editor of the *Augusta Chronicle*) asked Sherman why he spared the city and in an October 21, 1888, letter—published in the *Confederate Veteran* 22 (August 1914): 369—Sherman mentioned his concern that the Confederates had fortified both Augusta and Macon; he did not mention a woman.

12. Connolly, *Three Years*, 334.

13. "Why Sherman Snubbed Augusta," *Confederate Veteran* 22 (August 1914): 369.

14. Diary entries for November 11, 17, and 18, 1864, in Sneden, *Eye of the Storm*, 264, 271.

15. Diary entry for November 22, 1864, ibid., 272.

16. Ibid.; *O.R.* 44, 876.

17. Davis, *Jefferson Davis, Constitutionalist*, 6:407, 408, 421.

18. *Reminiscences of the Civil War from Diaries of Members of the 103d Illinois Volunteer Infantry*, 158–59, 161.

19. Davis, *Jefferson Davis, Constitutionalist*, 6:355, 413; John B. Jones, *A Rebel War Clerk's Diary*, 2 vols. (Philadelphia: J. B. Lippincott & Co., 1866), 2:342; D. H. Blair to "Dear Sister," November 20 [30], 1864, David Humphrey Blair Papers, 45th Ohio Infantry, Civil War Misc. Collection, USAMHI.

20. Andrews, *War-time Journal*, 32, 38.

21. *O.R.* 44, 412.

22. Ibid., 408; Connolly, *Three Years*, 335.

23. *O.R.* 44, 412; Connolly, *Three Years*, 345.

24. Connolly, *Three Years*, 345; *O.R.* 44, 585, 601.

25. *O.R.* 44, 624.

26. Connolly, *Three Years*, 329.

27. Noah Andre Trudeau, *Like Men of War: Black Troops in the Civil War, 1862–1865* (New York: Little, Brown & Co., 1998), 325, 328, 330; *O.R.* 44, 416.

28. Trudeau, *Like Men of War*, 330–31.

29. *Savannah Republican*, September 21 and November 19, 1864.

30. Ibid., November 26 and 30, 1864. The proclamation was issued on November 28.

31. Ibid., December 1, 1864.

32. Ibid., December 2, 3, 4, 13, 16, and 19, 1864.

33. Jones, *Siege of Savannah*, 74.

CHAPTER SEVEN

"ALMOST STARVED AND RAGGED"
Nearing Savannah

SHERMAN'S LEFT WING reached Millen the first week of December, but nothing remained at nearby Camp Lawton except a sign that read "650 buried here"—a telling indictment of conditions in a compound used for barely a month. A chaplain who inspected the abandoned facility recalled that it made his "heart ache" to see the "miserable hovels, hardly fit for swine to live in," which had served as housing for the prisoners. Every soldier who visited the stockade "came away with a hardness toward the Southern Confederacy he had never felt before." One man described it as a "hideous prison-pen." Even photographer George Barnard, who was along on the march and had commented that it disturbed him to see soldiers burn houses, after visiting Camp Lawton decided that the punishment of civilians who supported the Rebel government was justified. This elicited from Henry Hitchcock the response, "If B. feels so from *seeing* the prison pen, how do those feel who have suffered in it!" Angry soldiers set fire to Millen's train depot, and flames spread to the town, consuming some other buildings.[1]

The right wing also met little resistance in the lower part of the state. There was occasional skirmishing with Confederate cavalry; at Statesboro, Rebel horsemen as well as local militiamen halfheartedly tried to repel the invaders, but the casualties on both sides were light. Aside from such minor operations only one truly controversial event occurred during the march. It involved the contrabands who followed the Federal columns and placed so heavy a burden on the quartermasters' supplies.

Although the army had marched out of Atlanta with fewer than 200 escaped slaves, that number had grown to an estimated 10,000 by the time the wagons reached south Georgia. Entire families had fled their former masters. Some rode on mules, often crowding several children on one old animal; others came in wagons pulled by oxen or buggies taken from plantations. "Columns could be written descriptive of the harrowing scenes presented by this unfortunate

Burning the depot at Millen (*Harper's Weekly*)

class of fugitives," concluded one Northern newspaper. An Illinois soldier recorded in his diary, "An immense number of 'contrabands' now follow us, most of them able-bodied men, who intend going into the army." Moreover, as the army neared Savannah, the soldier observed that the numbers of refugees dramatically increased. On December 5 he recorded, "Negroes swarmed to us to-day. I saw one squad of 30 or 40 turned back. Sherman's order is not to let any more go with us than we can use and feed."[2]

Many Georgia slaves followed Sherman's army (USAMHI)

Not all soldiers approved of the decision to allow contrabands to follow the army, but even those who did were not prepared for the scores of refugees the march attracted as it crossed the state. One Wisconsin soldier complained that they were "a great hindrance, if not to say nuisance." Another judged that it would "start the tears on a pretty hard looking fase to see wih [sic] what joy our troops are greeted with by the poor down trodden slaves." An Indiana man believed that most of the refugees "realy don't seem to know just what freedom means," but a Minnesota soldier observed that the blacks were willing "to endure all the hardships of a long march to secure their liberty."[3]

The most notorious episode occurred as the army neared Savannah. Brigadier General Jefferson C. Davis, outspoken in his objections to the added mouths to feed, was a controversial personality. In Louisville, Kentucky, earlier in the war he had challenged his superior, 20-year navy veteran Major General William Nelson, to a duel. When Nelson refused, Davis shot him anyway, but was never brought to trial for murder because there were not enough officers available to form a court-martial. Instead, with the help of Indiana's governor, Davis received a transfer. He was not popular with the men in Georgia, particularly after he threatened to execute looters. He was, however, one of Sherman's favorites, even though one soldier complained that he thought the government was "hard up" when it allowed such men as Davis to command.[4]

Nevertheless, Davis led the Fourteenth Corps. At the end of the first week of December, his soldiers reached Ebenezer Creek, a swift, deep stream about 100 feet wide, not far from Savannah. Davis, known for negative opinions of black camp followers and his coarse vocabulary, ordered the contrabands out of the way as his men crossed on a pontoon bridge and left orders that only soldiers could use it.[5] Consequently, as the last trooper touched the southern riverbank, workers disassembled the bridge.

The blacks immediately sent up a collective "cry of agony," and when someone shouted "Rebels," men, women, and children panicked. Many plunged into the water, while others ran up and down the opposite bank shaking with terror. A Union private wrote that hundreds of refugees on the far creek bank "huddled as close to the edge of the water as they could get, some crying, some praying, and all fearful that the rebels would come before they could get over." Many drowned trying to swim the swollen stream, but others (according to Union soldiers) died at the hands of Rebel horsemen. Appalled Northern soldiers threw logs and tree branches to those in the water, and some black refugees ferried back across on a makeshift raft to rescue as many more as they could. A chaplain blasted Davis as "a military tyrant, without one spark of humanity in his makeup." A surgeon judged that if he had the power, he would see the general hanged. "I should not wonder," he concluded, "if the valiant murderer of women and children should meet with an accident before long."[6]

The incident quickly became the talk of the camps. "I heard tonight that General Davis turned back a lot of contrabands," penned one soldier. "I don't doubt it," he added, "for he is a copperhead." Another wrote, "Let the 'iron pen of history' write the comment on this action of a Union general." One observed that it was "a burning shame and a disgrace" to abandon the slaves, "for they prefer sinking in the water to returning to slavery." Indeed, judged another, "where can you find in all the annals of plantation cruelty anything more completely inhuman and fiendish than this?" Sherman, who had to answer for Davis's actions, endorsed the decision on the grounds of military necessity.[7]

Further, when the story eventually broke in Northern newspapers, General Davis initially appeared blameless, and criticism was leveled at Wheeler's cavalry. One reporter claimed that Wheeler's troopers had charged the contrabands, driving them mercilessly into the water and watching women and children drown. The writer did admit that he might have exaggerated for the sake of a good story: "How far true this may be I know not," he wrote, "but all the negroes who escaped, with whom I have talked, seem to agree in their account of the hellish slaughter." As soon as one officer reached Savannah, he composed a letter that appeared in a New York paper, criticizing Davis's deed, and later noted with pleasure that Davis was passed over for promotion to brevet major general. Davis's lack of promotion, however, probably resulted from his killing of General Nelson rather than his actions in south Georgia.[8]

Certainly, former slaves roaming the countryside worried Confederates, but when Wheeler did apprehend any, he generally returned them to those he still considered their owners. He admitted shelling the Fourteenth Corps "with good effect" during the night of December 8, causing the Yankees to abandon clothing, arms, and other goods they could not gather up and to desert a "great many negroes." One black told a Union soldier, "I am too old to go with you's, and I am too young to stay here an' be murdered." There was good reason for the slaves to fear retribution if caught by the Rebels, for punishment would certainly follow if they were returned to their former owners. During the weeks that the Confederates followed Sherman's wagon trains, Wheeler estimated that he apprehended nearly 2,000 blacks. Whether or not he restored all of these men, women, and children to their homes is unknown, for he crossed into South Carolina as soon as Sherman neared Savannah.[9]

Wheeler's instructions were to protect the route into Savannah from the north, on the South Carolina side of the river, a decision that left no defenders between Sherman and the city. There were several Confederate generals in the state, but few real soldiers. In fact, one available full general not ordered to the southeast coast was Joseph E. Johnston, who had only recently left Georgia after being replaced by Hood in July. So when Beauregard published a proclamation saying he would "rescue" Georgia, John B. Jones, a war clerk in Richmond, quipped, "Here, then, will be war between the two B.'s—Bragg and Beauregard; and the President will be as busy as a bee." The next day Jones added that Johnston had arrived in Richmond, regarded as a martyr to those who opposed President Davis's decision to remove him from command outside Atlanta. "If Sherman's campaign should be a success, Johnston will be a hero," noted Jones; "if the reverse, he will sink to rise no more. A sad condition," he decided, "for one's greatness to depend upon calamity to his country!"[10]

In Washington, meanwhile, Lincoln and Grant had no good idea of Sherman's location. Lincoln, addressing Congress on December 6, announced that Sherman's march was the "most remarkable" event of the year but acknowledged that there had been no communication with his army. Grant even joked that "Sherman's army is now somewhat in the condition of a ground-mole when he disappears under a lawn" or a western prairie dog: "You can here and there trace his track, but you are not quite certain where he will come out till you see his head."[11]

By this time, however, Georgians had concluded that Sherman's objective was Savannah. Even the general's men finally knew that the port city was their goal, but that knowledge did not lessen their fascination with the landscape of south Georgia. As the wagons neared the ocean, rice fields appeared, and swampy marshes hosted alligators and snakes. Soldiers who had never seen the coast surveyed it all with amazement. An Illinois soldier complained on December 11: "This is a country of awful swamps, with level flats, between which are rice fields, and most of them have three feet of water on them. . . . It is as much as we can do to find dry land enough to camp on." As evening approached, the man added, "It is quite cold again; to-night promises to be [the] coldest night of the winter." An officer recalled that "the country ceased to respond to the foragers' efforts, because they did not consider rice worth the risk and labor of getting."[12]

Sherman's concerns shifted as he neared the ocean. He feared strong opposition at Savannah, for he had heard rumors that Lee had sent Longstreet to reinforce the city. But although he did not know what awaited him, he certainly knew what lay behind. As food and forage dwindled daily, Sherman never considered turning back. He had to link up with the Union navy and the supplies that Washington had shipped south. On December 10 an officer complained, "How long will it take us to get over the *last* five of our '300 mile march?' " He feared that the food reserves would not hold out; if the army did not communicate with the fleet soon, the men and animals would "be pinched." A few days later the same officer observed that there were enough rations for the men for ten days, but forage for the horses, mules, and cattle had dropped substantially; even the corn and oats carried in the wagons had dwindled, and shortages began to affect everyone. A foot soldier pointedly observed that he was "almost starved and ragged. My shoes have given out and I am as good as barefooted with many others."[13]

Approaching the Atlantic was one thing; finding the U.S. Navy was another. Sherman gave Oliver O. Howard, whose right wing marched nearer the coast, this assignment, and Howard sent 23-year-old William Duncan, an Illinois captain, and two of his friends to make contact with the fleet. When there was no news for several days, Howard assumed that Duncan had failed. The three men had located a Union gunboat, however, and, after giving his message to Major General John G. Foster at Hilton Head, Duncan continued to Washington, where he personally delivered a second note to Secretary of War Edwin Stanton. On December 15 a New York newspaper announced, "At last the curtain has risen on the grand military drama in Georgia, and we are again in direct communication with the army of General Sherman." In his note, Howard had written, "We have met with perfect success thus far. Troops in fine spirits, and near by."[14]

Sherman's prize, the city of Savannah, was defended by a small army under General William J. Hardee. Nearly fifty years old, Hardee had served as commandant of cadets at West Point and was the author of a widely read textbook on military tactics. He was also a Georgian, and his family's plantation, called Rural Felicity, was near the Georgia coast. Hardee had assumed command of the Department of South Carolina, Georgia, and Florida in September. When Sherman left Atlanta, Hardee had traveled to Macon and points nearby to survey the situation, but he always knew that his main concern would be to protect the city of Savannah.

Local residents had followed the progress of Sherman with detached interest. Just a few days after he left Atlanta, the *Savannah Republican* had headlined, "What Sherman is Doing!" and cited "reliable information" from the *Chicago Times* that Sherman was about to do something "rather startling than otherwise." The Northern paper claimed that Sherman, "after gathering sufficient supplies at Atlanta," intended to "*march* with a strictly movable column on a winter tour of the Cotton States." And the local reporter pointed out, "This is an item of intelligence that may be safely classed under the head of 'important if true.' "[15]

Even though rumors abounded, the Savannah paper reassured concerned residents. Reports indicated that Sherman had been repulsed around Clinton in Jones County, and the trains between Macon and Savannah intended to "run through to-day, as usual." In any case, although the mayor issued an official warning for the residents to prepare but not to panic, most townspeople continued to hope that Augusta was the target.[16]

Although local residents tried to ignore Sherman, General Hardee continued to prepare. He succeeded in gathering some 10,000 defenders, even though few men were regular Confederate soldiers. As Sherman neared the city, Hardee became concerned about his ability to hold out. He wired Beauregard, who had just arrived in Charleston, that he wanted to talk. "It is," he stressed, "all important that I should confer with you."[17]

Beauregard, too, recognized the dire situation. He knew critics would ask why the Rebel army had left Georgia virtually defenseless, so from Augusta he wrote President Davis to enumerate his reasons for not countermanding Hood's march into Tennessee.

Beauregard explained that once Hood had gone into Alabama, it would have been impossible for him to return to Georgia. The wet, cold weather had made the roads across Alabama impassable for artillery and supply wagons, and those railroads actually running were in such poor condition as to cause unavoidable delays. Moreover, to return to Georgia would have seemed like a desperate action, a "retrograde movement" through a devastated country short of supplies, and would have resulted in the desertion of large numbers of men. Beauregard also argued that if Hood had not gone on the offensive, then the Union forces under George Thomas would have, and Montgomery, Selma, and Mobile would have been lost. To exonerate himself in the current situation, Beauregard pointed to Governor Brown's earlier declaration that he could raise enough troops to defend his state. On the basis of this assessment, Beauregard concluded that Confederate forces could reach as high as 30,000, while he incorrectly estimated Sherman's at only 36,000. He was wrong on both counts. The Confederates had only a fraction of his estimate, whereas Sherman had almost twice as many men as Beauregard thought.[18]

Of immediate concern to Hardee were the soldiers only 6 miles from the vital railway bridge across the Savannah River, the structure that provided the only link to the outside world. Beauregard had already told Hardee that there would be little chance of reinforcements and that if the Georgian had to make a choice between his army and the city, he should sacrifice the latter. Therefore, Beauregard ordered Hardee to construct a pontoon bridge across the river into South Carolina. Like Johnston before him, he was willing to give up land in Georgia and the city he was defending in order to preserve the army intact.[19]

Hardee's commanders had varying degrees of experience. Ambrose "Rans" Wright, commanding the left of Hardee's line, had been born near Augusta and settled there as an adult. He had led a brigade under Robert E. Lee and, although court-martialed for "disobedience towards superior officers" after Gettysburg, had handled his own defense and been acquitted. Wright then temporarily turned to politics. In the autumn of 1863 he was elected to the Georgia state senate, and left the army until the legislature adjourned. Although he returned to the Virginia theater, a minor illness forced him home again in 1864. He had been promoted to major general upon reaching Augusta, and he soon joined Hardee at Savannah.

Contemporaries described him as "too self-willed and combative" with "too much dash" and not enough "coolness."[20]

Gustavus W. Smith commanded the right of Hardee's line. Smith had graduated from West Point eighth in his class of fifty-six and later taught at the academy, but he resigned from the army in the mid-1850s. Smith's most notable hour came in 1862 when Joseph E. Johnston was wounded at the battle of Seven Pines during the Peninsular Campaign. He had briefly assumed command of the Confederate army, but an attack of paralysis, a mysteriously recurring malady that occasionally rendered him unfit for duty, forced him to pass the army to Lee. This undiagnosed disorder caused some to claim that Smith's immobility was brought on by knowing he could never live up to his own grandiose boasts. Described as "tall, burly, and unashamedly smug," he was no doubt convinced that the Confederacy did not appreciate his abilities. He resigned from the Confederate army early in 1863 after being passed over for promotion. He served briefly as secretary of war, but his inability to get along with President Davis had thrown him into the Beauregard camp, where he was a volunteer aide-de-camp before becoming major general of the Georgia militia in 1864. His performance during the Atlanta campaign brought neither recognition nor censure, but he seemed to function well enough when under the command of someone else. As the campaign for Savannah opened, Smith did have the distinction of having just returned from the battle at Honey Hill, where the militia had been victorious.[21]

At the center of the line was Augusta-born Lafayette McLaws. He had attended the University of Virginia before graduating from West Point in 1842. He was a career U.S. Army officer but resigned to join the Confederate army when the war came. McLaws fought at Sharpsburg, Fredericksburg, Chancellorsville, and Gettysburg. At Gettysburg he had become angry with James Longstreet, who was not only his commander but also an old acquaintance from the military academy. McLaws called Longstreet "a humbug, a man of small capacity, very obstinate, not at all chivalrous, exceedingly conceited, and totally selfish." Not surprisingly, the two men had an argument several weeks later, and Longstreet brought several charges against his old friend following the failed Knoxville campaign. Davis, however, sided with McLaws and Longstreet was the one to draw censure from the War Department. Yet it was McLaws who received a transfer to the west. He was particularly suited to defend against a siege outside Savannah, for he had begun his Confederate career in that seaport and had later earned a reputation in the Army of Northern Virginia for his defense. A staff officer recalled the general as "fond of detail," and an artilleryman judged that McLaws was "about the best general in the army for that sort of job."[22]

Hardee had done everything he could to prepare the city's defenses, but as Sherman's columns approached and the Confederates withdrew from the outer perimeter, he had to destroy the Savannah & Charleston Railroad bridge. On December 11 he informed Beauregard, "I have been obliged to extend my line. It is impossible to hold it without immediate reenforcement." Unfortunately, Beauregard could offer only a few units, nothing near the number Hardee needed. After Union gunners fired on Confederate vessels north of the city, Hardee feared that Sherman might challenge him along the river. To eliminate any threat from South Carolina, he had already ordered Wheeler to withdraw from Sherman's rear and move the cavalry to Hardeeville, on the South Carolina side of the river, in order to protect the crossings. Still, once Slocum's men had taken an island in the river, Hardee knew that if Sherman pressed this advantage by moving more than a regiment onto the island, the Federals could block his retreat.[23]

Nevertheless, the city still presented a challenge for Sherman. The coastal terrain favored defenders, for Savannah lay between rivers: the inland peninsula was about 13 miles wide, with the Savannah River on the north and the Little Ogeechee River on the south. To the west, Hardee ordered the rice fields flooded; some 3 to 6 feet of water created a muddy mess. In spite of the flooded fields, the danger still lay to the west and, to a lesser degree, to the south, where Fort McAllister had protected the entrance to Ossabaw Sound and the Ogeechee River since early in the war.

Hardee understood strategy as well as any soldier on either side, and he knew that Sherman's first objective was not the city itself. Well aware of how many weeks Sherman had been on the road, he also knew that the sparsely settled pine woods of southeast Georgia offered little food or forage. The knowledge that Sherman would hit McAllister first gave Hardee a little more time to prepare, but that time could not be gained without sacrifice. The fort's 200 defenders fell outside Hardee's defensive perimeter, even though McAllister was Savannah's last line of defense before Sherman reached the city's earthworks. The fort also offered the only obstacle between Sherman's 60,000 hungry men and the supply ships along the coast. That spelled disaster for the Confederates who manned the guns in the isolated stronghold.

NOTES

1. Burke Davis, *Sherman's March* (1980; reprint, New York: Vintage Books, 1988), 88; Glatthaar, *March to the Sea*, 77; Nichols, *Story of the Great March*, 84; Hitchcock, *Marching with Sherman*, 150.

2. *New York Herald*, December 22, 1864; *Reminiscences of the Civil War from Diaries of Members of the 103d Illinois Volunteer Infantry*, 162, 164.

3. Glatthaar, *March to the Sea*, 53.

4. Ibid., 22.

5. Connolly, *Three Years*, 354–55.

6. Davis, *Sherman's March*, 92–93; James P. Jones, "General Jeff C. Davis, U.S.A., and Sherman's Georgia Campaign," *Georgia Historical Quarterly* 47 (March 1962): 243. See also Carlin, *Memoirs*, 157–58, for another account of the incident.

7. Connolly, *Three Years*, 347; Glatthaar, *March to the Sea*, 64; Davis, *Sherman's March*, 92–94.

8. *New York Herald*, December 22, 1864.

9. *O.R.* 44, 410; Kennett, *Marching through Georgia*, 293.

10. Jones, *A Rebel War Clerk's Diary*, 2:340–42.

11. Davis, *Sherman's March*, 89; Porter, *Campaigning with Grant*, 332–33.

12. *Reminiscences of the Civil War from Diaries of Members of the 103d Illinois Volunteer Infantry*, 167; Carlin, *Memoirs*, 155.

13. Hitchcock, *Marching with Sherman*, 166, 172, 176; John Rath, *Left for Dixie: The Civil War Diary of John Rath*, ed. Kenneth Lyftogt (Parkersburg, IA: Mid-Prairie Books, 1991), 64.

14. *New York Herald*, December 15, 1864; *O.R.* 44, 676.

15. *Savannah Republican*, November 18, 1864.

16. Ibid., November 19, 21, and 26, 1864.

17. Nathaniel Cheairs Hughes Jr., *General William J. Hardee: Old Reliable* (1965; reprint, Baton Rouge: Louisiana State University Press, 1992), 258.

18. *O.R.* 44, 932.

19. Ibid., 940.

20. Keith P. Bohannon, "Ambrose Ransom Wright," in Davis, *Confederate Generals*, 6:161, 163.

21. Lesley Jill Gordon-Burr, "Gustavus W. Smith," in Current, *Encyclopedia of the Confederacy*, 4:1474.

22. Robert K. Krick, "Lafayette McLaws," in Current, *Encyclopedia of the Confederacy*, 3:974.

23. Hughes, *General William J. Hardee*, 261.

CHAPTER EIGHT

"I REGARD SAVANNAH
AS ALREADY GAINED"
The City's Defenses

FORT MCALLISTER STOOD on the Ogeechee River, 7 miles from the Atlantic Ocean and 12 miles below Savannah. Designed in 1861 and named for a local landowner, it protected plantations in the area, as well as the routes into the city from the south, including an important bridge of the Atlantic & Gulf Railroad. McAllister was a heavily armed earthen fortification. Even the river was mined with torpedoes to keep enemy ships at a distance. Unlike the masonry walls of Fort Pulaski, which had been blasted through by Federal fire in the spring of 1862, McAllister had survived two attacks later that same summer. In November 1862 an ironclad fired more than 100 shells into the fort before Confederate gunners forced it to withdraw. In fact, throughout the war, McAllister weathered several attacks with little damage, for the earthworks generally absorbed the shells and could be quickly repaired. After a failed naval assault in 1863, Union authorities decided that the fort was impregnable. Even Horace Greeley later wrote, "From this time the Union fleet saved their ammunition by letting McAllister alone."[1]

Unfortunately for Savannah, though, McAllister's heavy guns faced the water rather than land and would be useless against an infantry attack. Only twelve cannon, unprotected by earthworks, covered the fort's rear. Still, Major George W. Anderson, who commanded the 200 defenders, had ordered the construction of a high earthen wall, and there was also a ditch 15 feet deep and 7 feet wide, with pointed logs protruding from the center. An abatis of tree limbs surrounded the fort, and Anderson had placed land torpedoes in the marshes and fields outside its perimeter. Yet nothing could change the fact that the defenders were overwhelmingly outnumbered.

Storming fortifications had never been Sherman's style. Neither was a siege. But he needed to open communications with the fleet, so he wasted no time in making arrangements to take the fort, selecting William B. Hazen's division of the Fifteenth Corps for the attack. These were men from the Army of the Tennessee, and he had confidence in these western soldiers. As they prepared for the assault on December 13, Sherman watched from the roof of a shed at a rice mill nearby. He knew the odds were in his favor, for Hazen had more than 4,000 men. Even the 3,000 that actually participated outnumbered the defenders fifteen to one.

Fort McAllister (Library of Congress)

Luck was also on the Union side. Just about the time the attack was scheduled to open, an officer with Sherman sighted a vessel flying a U.S. flag. Sherman immediately instructed his signalmen to make contact while he turned his attention to the scene unfolding at the fort. As the daylight hours dimmed, Sherman lost patience with delay after delay and reminded Hazen that he wanted the fort subdued before dark. That nudge was enough to get Hazen moving, and when he ordered the charge, scores of men rushed forward. One officer watched the line materialize from the woods, press forward in a solid mass, and with fixed bayonets march up the causeway to the outer work. They did not fire a shot, even though they were exposed to a heavy and constant cannonade. Then, with some twenty regimental flags flying in the breeze, they charged the main work. Presently the head of the column sank from view, and for a moment Sherman feared that the assault had been repulsed. Then he saw the line reemerge up a hill, reach the parapet, and pour into the fort. The onlookers in Sherman's party cheered, grasping hands and embracing. The general later told his wife that watching his old division take McAllister was the "handsomest thing" he had seen in the war.[2]

Attack on Fort McAllister (*Harper's Weekly*)

The fighting, though lasting less than twenty minutes, was brutal. Major Anderson later commended the gallant conduct of Captain Nicholas B. Clinch, whose fight with the officer who demanded his surrender had stopped only after some Union privates came to their commander's assistance. Clinch's "cool bravery" elicited praise even from Sherman. The hospital at Beaufort later reported that Clinch had suffered a bayonet strike and gunshot to his left arm, three saber wounds in the back, four saber wounds in the scalp,

and a fractured skull but seemed to have a "fair prospect of recov-
ering." On the Federal side, Captain Stephen F. Grimes of the Forty-
eighth Illinois was commended for his conduct in the battle (his
sharpshooters silenced two of the 10-inch guns) and for his hand-
to-hand fight with Clinch. Major Anderson later insisted that
McAllister "never surrendered. It was captured by overwhelming
numbers." After the fort fell, a Union soldier predicted, "We will
have Savannah, sure."[3]

Fort McAllister in Union hands (Library of Congress)

McAllister netted the Federals twenty-four guns, one mortar,
sixty tons of ammunition, food, and various arms and supplies.
Some wine found in the storehouses particularly pleased the victors. The Union lost twenty-four men killed and had over 100
wounded. The Confederates had seventeen killed and around thirty
wounded; the remainder became prisoners of war. The unfortu-

nate Confederates also had the unpleasant and dangerous task of removing the land mines that had been carefully hidden in the sand. Sherman had already strongly criticized the Confederate decision to plant the shells in the ground with "friction-matches" that made them explode on contact, declaring, "This was not war, but murder, and it made me very angry." When some prisoners begged not to be asked to clear the road, Sherman forced them to remove the explosives; he noted that one "could hardly help laughing at their stepping so gingerly along the road, where it was supposed sunken torpedoes might explode at each step."[4]

Sherman immediately wrote Secretary of War Stanton that "the army is in splendid order, and equal to anything." He exaggerated slightly when he added, "Our march was most agreeable, and we were not at all molested by guerrillas. . . . We have not lost a wagon on the trip, but have gathered a large supply of negroes, mules, horses, &c., and our teams are in far better condition than when we started." He also noted, "We have utterly destroyed over 200 miles of rails, and consumed stores and provisions that were essential to Lee's and Hood's armies." Never at a loss for confidence, he ended by bluntly stating, "I regard Savannah as already gained."[5]

A letter to Henry Halleck was equally optimistic. Sherman repeated what he had told Edwin Stanton, then began to campaign for permission to march through the Carolinas. "I can only say that I hope by Christmas to be in possession of Savannah," he wrote, "and by the new year to be ready to resume our journey to Raleigh. The whole army is crazy to be turned loose in Carolina; and with the experience of the past thirty days I judge that a month's sojourn in South Carolina would make her less bellicose." Sherman was fully aware of the psychological damage he had done. "The editors in Georgia profess to be indignant at the horrible barbarities of Sherman's army, but I know the people don't want our visit repeated. . . . A similar destruction of roads and resources hence to Raleigh would compel General Lee to come out of his intrenched camp."[6]

The fall of McAllister resulted in celebration within the Union lines. "We all breathe freer to-night than we have for three months past," wrote Major James A. Connolly. With McAllister under Union control, hungry troops knew the army could now contact the fleet for supplies. The diet of rice, without meat or crackers and but little coffee or sugar, had become wearisome. The rice was still in the straw, and the soldiers had to do their own threshing before they could get enough for a meal, while the horses and mules had been reduced to eating rice straw.[7]

Communication with the fleet also allowed soldiers to hear from home. Brigadier General John W. Geary, like thousands of other men, immediately wrote his family of his recent exploits. "Yesterday was a day racy and rare, and under all the circumstances long to be remembered," he told his wife, Mary. "We had been thirty-one days cut off from the world and 'the rest of mankind,' during which period we had not received a single word concerning the affairs of the North, except occasionally through the unreliable and lying *sheets* of the South, but yesterday we had a carnival of letters and newspapers." Predictably, official word of George McClellan's loss to Lincoln in November comforted the weary travelers. "The news of the presidential election was all fresh to us," he noted, "although we had learned, through rebel sources, of Mr. Lincoln's election."[8]

Sherman, however, wasted no time savoring his victory. He ordered heavy guns transported from Port Royal in South Carolina in preparation for an attack on the city but confided to his wife that he did not intend to assault Savannah. He wanted to starve civilians and soldiers into submission. Just days after McAllister fell, he had his brother-in-law, Charles Ewing, deliver a formal surrender demand to city officials. Sherman warned Hardee that if he was forced to take Savannah by assault, he would resort to "the harshest measures" and make little effort to restrain his army. Although this was only saber rattling, a Federal officer heard a rumor that Sherman intended to open the city to the men for two days without any restraints. To emphasize that he meant business, Sherman included a copy of Hood's October communication with the Union commander at Dalton, Georgia, in which the Texas general had threatened to give no quarter if he was compelled to carry the place by assault. A Union officer who knew what was going on wrote, "General Hardee replied that he declined to surrender, and that in the conduct of the war he had always been governed by the usage of civilized nations. They were both 'only talking,' and both knew it."[9]

Even with McAllister in Union hands, taking Savannah without a siege provided Sherman with a perplexing and dangerous problem. The interminable swamps of the Low Country were the city's salvation, for the only way to cross them was on narrow causeways. The general admitted to Ellen that he had almost been wounded while scouting the Confederate defenses, and a "negros head was shot off close by me." John Geary noted, "The enemy have a strong line in our front, well defended with swamp dykes, rice-field marshes." The Rebels were also "very defiant. We are therefore in the midst of the thunders of a siege." Savannah, he judged, was a "great prize, and like all things of great value, very difficult to obtain."[10]

Confederate fortifications at Savannah (National Archives)

Union prisoner Robert Knox Sneden, who had been incarcerated in a stockade attached to the Chatham County jail which held around 5,000 prisoners, had written in September, "The city itself looked beautiful embowered in trees, with the numerous church steeples clear against a cloudless sky." He even remarked on the charity of the citizens: "Several boxes of provisions and some good clothing [were] sent into the stockade by the Masonic fraternity of the city," he reported, "but those who were Masons got them after an equal division. Hams, pies, fruit, etc. made the recipients happy for days." After being transferred to Millen, Sneden heard that General McLaws had ordered the stockade destroyed "so that he would never have so many prisoners of war in his city again." Although his remarks about McLaws were secondhand, Sneden did point out later that the prison pen was gone when he returned to the city in late November.[11]

Having signed a parole to work for a Confederate surgeon while in prison at Millen, Sneden enjoyed the sights of Savannah on that second visit. His quarters, as well as the doctor's, were in the Screven House, a hotel that had replaced the older Pulaski House as the most fashionable in Savannah but "was now devoid of furniture or occupants." When the doctor told him he could stay anywhere, Sneden moved to the Pulaski House, paying $38 per day in Confederate money, "not exorbitant taking into consideration that it took twenty of [their dollars] to make one greenback of our money," and remarking, "Board was to be had there from $40 to $60 per day!" He noted that meals at the Pulaski House were excellent, "though corn meal and rice, sweet potatoes and ham formed the principal dishes."[12]

Savannah in November 1864, the Union soldier judged, was captivating. "The buildings were fine throughout the city, and much more architectural than those of Richmond." Huge piles of cotton sat at the depot of the Charleston Railroad waiting for transportation that would have eventually taken the bales by blockade runners to England. He heard "there was about 50,000 bales of cotton in the city."[13] Even as Sherman neared Savannah, life had continued as usual. Sneden observed, "There is an open market here, where Negro hucksters abound, and who bring their vegetables, etc. in by small carts driven by mules." But on November 26 "a raid was made by the [Confederate] military on the premises, and all the Negroes there found were impressed to work on the fortifications." Frightened blacks fled, and "mule teams were running away without drivers, spilling vegetables and other articles through the streets." The provost guard even forced white citizens to work on the fortifications.[14]

In short, Savannah had felt little direct effect of the war until November. True, prices had risen, and Sneden complained that because "oysters were $1 apiece, or $7 per plate, rye coffee $3 per cup (Confederate) I could not keep eating very long at this rate." But after a mulatto barber learned his patron was a paroled Yankee, he received a $10.00 shave free in an "elegantly fitted up" shop with "marble, glass, and gilt frescoes, etc." Moreover, Sneden noted the existence of a loyal "Union League" in the city.[15]

As Sneden left the city on a train bound for Charleston, he observed travelers singing " 'We'll hang Abe Lincoln to a sour apple tree' in maudlin tones," and the band played the "Bonnie Blue Flag" and other patriotic melodies. Yet Sneden also commented that "many of the prominent men were leaving for Wilmington or going south to St. Augustine, Florida to be out of Yankee reach." Skirmishing near the railroad at Pocotaligo in South Carolina and the appearance of Union gunboats could only mean that Union troops were drawing closer, and the exodus escalated. Hardee knew that Confederate horsemen could not hold the roads open long, and he needed to move quickly if he wanted to save his army.[16]

To evacuate the trenches outside the city and cross the river, Hardee instructed Brigadier General Pierce M. B. Young to collect rice flats and construct a makeshift bridge to the opposite riverbank. Young was a South Carolinian who had grown up in Georgia and had attended the Georgia Military Institute. Later he went to West Point, but the war prevented him from graduating because he left the academy to join the Confederate army. He had fought with the Army of Northern Virginia before being ordered to Georgia to assist Hardee. As Young oversaw the construction of the pontoon bridge, many residents packed their meager belongings and made plans to leave with the army. It took three separate links to connect the islands with the South Carolina shore, some thirty rice flats, each 70 to 80 feet long, making up the bridge. They had to be strapped together and then covered with wood taken from nearby wharves. Because of the scarcity of flats, the engineers tied them together end to end and not side by side as was typical. Georgia militiamen, sailors, and slaves composed the work parties.[17]

This would be a Christmas unlike any that Georgians had seen before. Instead of hosting gracious parties with festive holiday trimmings, numerous families abandoned their Christmas decorations and, with only scant possessions, fled the city. The authorities softened the sound of hundreds of wagons and carriages crossing the pontoon bridge by using rice straw as a muffler. Slaves coaxed balky horses and mules onto the shaking structure; frightened animals had to be blindfolded before they could be persuaded to advance. Women and children often walked, for their wagons were filled with everything they could pack. Some Union soldiers on the South

Carolina shore watched, but no one made any attempt to stop the procession; everyone assumed that someone else would prevent the flight. Additionally, Sherman had left explicit instructions that nothing should happen before he returned from a brief trip to South Carolina.

The military evacuation of Savannah was a poignant sight. One Confederate noted, "The constant tread of the troops and the rumblings of the artillery as they poured over those long floating bridges was a sad sight, and by the glare of the large fires at the east of the bridge it seemed like an immense funeral procession stealing out of the city in the dead of night." Another soldier told his mother, "I have no words to picture the gloomy bitterness that filled my breast on that dreary march through water, mud and darkness." By this time, it was impossible for the Federals not to realize that something significant was happening, for fires of abandoned and burned Rebel vessels lit the night skies.[18] The retreating Confederates wanted to be sure that when Sherman did occupy the city, there would be nothing there he could use, so as they withdrew from the defensive perimeter, they destroyed ammunition, spiked old or damaged cannons, and removed any weapons still in serviceable condition. They also burned Fort Jackson's barracks, spiked the citadel's guns, and demolished the gun carriages.

Confederate soldiers crossing the Savannah River (*Harper's Weekly*)

Federal soldiers were unaware of the panic gripping the Confederates; on December 20, exactly one week after the fall of Fort McAllister and four years to the day since South Carolina seceded, a soldier wrote, "Another quiet day; but the bustle of preparation for the assault can be seen on all hands, and everybody feels confident of the result." The following morning, however, men in the Union camps heard the cry "Savannah is evacuated." One officer recalled: "In less time than it takes to tell it, the heaviest sleepers in the army, as well as the lightest, were out, some dressed, and some *en deshabille*, shouting and hurrahing from the bottom of their lungs. This was indeed a joyful morning. Savannah is ours. Our long campaign is ended." Charles Wills, another Union soldier, added, "We have just by a hair's breadth missed what would have been a most unpleasant fight." At the same time, Confederate Willy Gordon entered in his diary, *"Savannah evacuated last night. . . .* This seventh anniversary of my wedding day ends seven happy years! The future is very dark."[19]

John W. Geary, seen here with his staff, to whom the mayor surrendered the city (Library of Congress)

Unfortunately, Sherman had missed the most important day of the campaign. Anticipating a siege, he had left for Hilton Head Island to discuss his options with Admiral John A. Dahlgren of the Navy and General John G. Foster, who commanded the Department of the South. After spending Tuesday at Hilton Head making preparations for his next move, Sherman was delayed in his return to Georgia when Dahlgren's flagship ran aground during a storm. The general did not hear that Hardee had evacuated Savannah until a tug arrived to pull the vessel out of the mud bank left by the low tide.

With the army gone, only civilians remained to surrender the city. Mayor Richard Arnold and several aldermen rode out the Louisville Road in search of a Union officer, and pickets escorted them

to John Geary. As soon as Geary agreed to protect the citizens and
their private property, the first occupation troops, men from Henry
Barnum's brigade of Geary's division, arrived. The last Confederates, those who had remained behind to destroy the bridges, barely
escaped. Moreover, the only defiant action came from a Rebel ironclad: when the U.S. flag appeared above Fort Jackson, the Rebel
sailors harmlessly shelled the old masonry bastion. Federal attempts
to sink the vessel failed, but the Confederates abandoned it shortly
after dark, leaving it to burn in the middle of the river. Around
midnight, when it finally exploded, the blast shook windows at
Hilton Head, some 20 miles away.

Although Savannah was now at the mercy of an enemy army,
General Geary moved quickly to prevent looting. He placed a guard
at the Masonic Hall and at the same time ordered the U.S. flag raised
over the City Exchange. Within a few days, more than 700 citizens
voted to rejoin the Union, and soon men from both sides were so-
cializing at the Freemasons' Lodge. Savannah was back in the
Union.[20]

NOTES

1. Miles, *To the Sea*, 287.
2. Hitchcock, *Marching with Sherman*, 179–80; Nichols, *Story of the Great March*, 91; Sherman, *Sherman's Civil War*, 767.
3. William R. Scaife, "Sherman's March to the Sea," *Blue and Gray Magazine* 7 (December 1989): 40; *O.R.* 44, 122; Wills, *Army Life*, 335; Jones, *Siege of Savannah*, 127.
4. Sherman, *Memoirs*, 2:194.
5. *O.R.* 44, 701.
6. Ibid., 702.
7. Connolly, *Three Years*, 362.
8. John White Geary, *A Politician Goes to War: The Civil War Letters of John White Geary*, ed. William Alan Blair (University Park: Pennsylvania State University Press, 1995), 217.
9. Sherman, *Sherman's Civil War*, 769; *O.R.* 44, 737; Thomas Ward Osborne, *The Fiery Trail: A Union Officer's Account of Sherman's Last Campaigns*, eds. Richard Harwell and Philip N. Racine (Knoxville: University of Tennessee Press, 1986), 72.
10. Sherman, *Sherman's Civil War*, 768; Geary, *Civil War Letters*, 216, 218.
11. Sneden, *Eye of the Storm*, 258–59, 273.
12. Diary entries dated November 23, 24, and 25, 1864, ibid., 272–74.
13. Diary entry dated November 25, ibid., 274.
14. Diary entry dated November 26, 1864, ibid., 275.
15. Diary entries dated November 26 and 28, 1864, ibid., 276–77.
16. Diary entries dated November 26 and 29, 1864, ibid., 275, 279.

17. Jones, *Siege of Savannah*, 133–34.

18. Roger S. Durham, "Savannah: Mr. Lincoln's Christmas Present," *Blue and Gray Magazine* 8 (February 1991), 48; Henry Graves to "My Dearest Mother," December 28, 1864, United Daughters of the Confederacy Collection, Georgia Department of Archives and History, Atlanta, 6:341.

19. Connolly, *Three Years*, 368; Wills, *Army Life*, 335; entry dated December 21, 1864, William W. Gordon Diary, Gordon Family Papers, Southern Historical Collection, Louis Round Wilson Library, University of North Carolina, Chapel Hill.

20. Jones, *Siege of Savannah*, 163; Geary, *Civil War Letters*, 219.

"A Season of Sadness"
Savannah at Christmas

"THIS IS A BEAUTIFUL CITY and very old," wrote a Union soldier. Savannah showed no visible scars of war; there were no burned buildings or ravaged homes. When Sherman rode into town, he could hardly believe that years had passed since his last visit as a young army officer in the 1840s. The houses he remembered still survived untouched; only an unnatural silence spoke of the tension within the hushed and locked mansions that lined the fashionable squares. He wrote his son Tom, "I suppose Mama has told you all about my army travelling across Georgia and coming out on the ocean at the beautiful City of Savannah. You will find it in your Geography, but can hardly understand the importance of it till you are larger and older." As the endless procession of soldiers moved into the city, residents who had refused to leave or could not flee peeked out through shuttered windows. Savannahians knew that nothing could be done except watch as the squares and parks became military camps for jubilant occupation troops.[1]

For the Union soldiers, Christmas in 1864 was a time of both celebration and relaxation. "In 24 days we had marched from Atlanta to Savannah" and had "besieged the place for 11 days," wrote an officer. "A little rest was a grateful thing." Unlike soldiers in the Confederate Army of Tennessee, who marked the holidays retreating south after a devastating defeat at Nashville, Sherman's "bummers" enjoyed the peaceful tranquility of Savannah unmolested by enemy fire. Sightseeing proved a popular pastime. Bull Street, noted one Northerner, "had been a beautiful avenue, with a fine square planted in shrubbery at every alternate street-crossing. The paving stones had all been taken up and used in blockading the Savannah River, leaving the street a very sandy and unlovely passageway." A soldier added, "Savannah is considered one of the finest cities in the South, but I was greatly disappointed in it. . . . The streets instead of being nicely paved are two or three inches deep with heavy sand so that it is difficult to cross them." Furthermore, pronounced

another, "There are a great many beautiful buildings in it certainly
and some large stores but both stores and residences have an old
dilapidated appearance that makes one long to see again some of
the lively cities of the North." He added that businesses were open
and trade was "beginning to stand up quite brisk, but all for 'Green-
backs' in fact you couldn't buy a shoestring with a bucket of confederate notes." Yet everything was too high, he complained,
although "this will soon be regulated."[2]

Union soldiers parading in Savannah (*Leslie's Illustrated*)

Now that they were safely in Savannah, many soldiers looked
back on the past weeks with nostalgia. A New Yorker recalled that
on the march "we lived on the fat of the land—Sweet Potatoes, Pork,
Mutton, Poultry, Honey, Sugar, Syrup & all most any thing you
could desire. We did not draw Government rations enough on the
march to have last us a week if we had been in camp. We also got a
supply of splendid Mules & Horses which by the way we could
never have got through without as our old Atlanta ones were nearly
starved to death when we started." He told his sister, "I think this
'Savannah Campaign' has cost the least in men and material & accomplished the most of any campaign since the war commenced."
Still, it was a Christmas far from home, and a soldier from Missouri wrote in his diary, "Sprinkled rain this morning, a damp
cloudy day. I bought two dozen johnney crackers for 50¢. We had a
very poor Christmas."[3]

For Southerners, of course, the holiday period was a time of immense sorrow. One young woman wrote, "Christmas is here again. . . . A season of sadness & gloomy retrospection for us of the South, one of joy & gayety to the people of the North." Fanny Cohen confided to her diary: "This is the saddest Christmas that I have ever spent and my only pleasure during the day has been in looking forward to spending my next Christmas in the Confederacy."[4]

For Northerners across the continent, the holiday season was a time for rejoicing. Sherman presented the city of Savannah as a gift, along with 25,000 bales of cotton, to the Northern president three days before Christmas. The message actually arrived in Washington on Christmas Eve, and Northern newspapers reveled in Sherman's success, professing that no American would ever again buy a gift without recalling "the great soldier who has given this grandest of Christmas gifts to the country." The *New York Herald* predicted that the surrender of Savannah would cause Lee's soldiers to desert, and the rebellion would soon end.[5]

"Many, many thanks for your Christmas gift, the capture of Savannah," Lincoln told the general. "When you were about leaving Atlanta for the Atlantic coast, I was anxious, if not fearful," but "I did not interfere. Now, the undertaking being a success, the honor is all yours; for I believe none of us went further than to acquiesce." Sherman's strategy, Lincoln continued, was "indeed a great success. Not only does it afford the obvious and immediate military advantages, but, in showing to the world that your army could be divided, putting the stronger part to an important new service, and yet leaving enough to vanquish the old opposing force of the whole—Hood's army—it brings those who sat in darkness to see a great light."[6]

Although Sherman did not receive Lincoln's praise until after Christmas, he could still celebrate, content in the knowledge that he had succeeded. The general attended services at St. John's, an Episcopal church on Madison Square. A Victorian Gothic building, the church had been built in 1852 and, so legend goes, had its chimes saved from confiscation during the occupation through a special plea to President Lincoln. "I was delighted to see it filled," an officer wrote his wife, "not only by a large number of our officers and men, but also a considerable number of Savannah people, ladies and gentlemen." The rector, a Mr. McRae, was aided by a "Yankee Chaplain," noted a woman who attended the service. Sherman then had a relaxing evening at a dinner party with the family of his

host, Charles Green. The general had initially moved into the
Pulaski House, the hotel where he had stayed as an officer in the
old army. When Green offered his home instead, Sherman had refused until he learned that Green was a British subject.[7]

The Charles Green house, Sherman's Savannah headquarters (USAMHI)

The Green house on Madison Square was one of the most elegant in Savannah. The mansion had been constructed largely of
building materials brought from England. It was solid masonry with
a battlemented roof line and windows of the Victorian Gothic style,
but with intricate ironwork on the windows and balcony showing
a French influence. Sherman told Ellen, "I am at this moment in an
elegant chamber of the house of a Gentleman named Green. The
house is elegant & splendidly furnished with pictures & Statuary—
my bed Room has a bath & dressing Room attached which look out
of proportion to my poor baggage." Because the house belonged to
a foreigner, the U.S. government paid Green a token rent, and as
soon as other residents realized the safety in foreign citizenship,
foreign flags appeared over many buildings. One Prussian barber
renamed his establishment the Union Barber Shop. Still, Sherman
seized much cotton that foreigners claimed, and the 25,000 bales
he had tendered President Lincoln multiplied. In spite of protests,
the number of bales confiscated was estimated at nearly 40,000.[8]

Throughout the city, newly freed slaves gathered to see the famous general. Sherman wrote to Ellen, "It would amuse you to See

the negros, they flock to me old & young they pray & shout—and mix up my name with that of Moses, & Simon, and other scriptural ones as well as Abram Linkum the Great Messiah of 'Dis Jubilee.' "[9]

Former slaves on Cockspur Island near Savannah (USAMHI)

Washington wanted to be sure that Sherman was fair in his dealings with the city's black residents, as well as the contrabands that had followed his army. Before he marched into South Carolina, he would have a personal visit from Secretary of War Edwin Stanton, whose official reason for the trip was to reestablish Union control of the port city and investigate the cotton trade. But he also wanted explanations for the rumors concerning the army's treatment of the contrabands. Stanton talked with leading black ministers, who assured the secretary that Sherman had been fair in his dealings with the former slaves. Sherman, to prove his commitment to the end of bondage, issued Special Field Order No. 15, redistributing the land along the Georgia coast to freed slaves. The experiment along the Sea Islands was the general's solution to the "Negro nonsense": that is, the pressure to enroll black soldiers in his white army. This way, he argued, black men could stay home and take care of their families while becoming productive landowners.[10]

While Savannah's black population celebrated a newly found freedom, the white residents remained subdued even as conditions slowly returned to normal. Frances Howard entered in her diary on New Year's Eve, "The city authorities have seen fit to declare

the city once more in the Union." Sherman later wrote, "It was estimated that there were about twenty thousand inhabitants in Savannah, all of whom had participated more or less in the war and
had no special claims to our favor." But festive activities drew attention, and "the great bulk of the inhabitants chose to remain in
Savannah, [and] generally behaved with propriety, and good social relations at once arose between them and the army." When the
anxiety finally lifted, the "guard-mountings and parades, as well
as the greater reviews, became the daily resort of the ladies, to hear
the music of our excellent bands; schools were opened, and the
churches every Sunday were well filled with most devout and re-
spectful congregations; stores were reopened, and markets for provisions, meat, wood, etc., were established." He admitted privately
that he found the women "haughty, and proud as ever," but as he
told Ellen, "I think Thomas' whipping at Nashville, coupled with
my march will take Some conceit out of them."[11]

Sherman gave Confederate sympathizers the option of staying
in their homes or joining friends and families in other cities. He
visited the home of Nelly Gordon, whose family was from Illinois.
When he asked Nelly why she had not gone to live with her family
in the North, the young woman explained that she could not leave
without the consent of her husband, who had retreated across the
Savannah River with the army. To help Nelly, the general issued a
pass allowing her to visit her spouse in South Carolina. Brigadier
General William P. Carlin recorded in his memoirs that "a very accomplished and agreeable lady of Northern birth, but of Southern
adoption, had procured from General Sherman permission to visit
Charleston, where her husband was located in the Confederate service." Carlin had recently received a $100 Confederate note as a
souvenir—part of a $350,000 cache found buried outside Savannah
by men of the Eighty-eighth Indiana. Since the money was of no
use in Union-occupied Savannah but still valuable in Confederate-
controlled territory, "knowing that she contemplated this trip, I
offered her the Confederate note, saying that she might possibly
find it useful. The offer was accepted, and she told me after her
return that it served her well."[12]

Whether it was Nelly who took money from a Union officer or
not, an angry Willy Gordon wrote in his diary that he was "very,
very sorry N. came under the flag. . . . To see her going away under
their Flag, while all around me were C[onfederates] was like tear-
ing my heart out by the roots. It has haunted me like a nightmare

ever since & will to the end of the War or the end of my life." He was "humiliated, crushed, & stung" and told his wife, "What galls me is that you should associate with *my* enemies upon any other terms than those which politeness demands from every lady." Despite her husband's disapproval, Nelly subsequently joined her parents in Chicago. She took with her their three children.[13]

In fact, Sherman allowed around 200 people, mainly women and children whose husbands and fathers were in the Confederate army, to leave. Among the women who had remained in the city during the siege were the wives of William Hardee, Lafayette McLaws, Gustavus Smith, and A. P. Stewart. The general told Ellen that the "very elegant people" of the city did not seem "ashamed to call on the Vandal Chief" to request favors. Sherman also did not interfere with the mayor and city council; as one officer observed, an outsider would not notice that Savannah was "so lately a prize of battle." A soldier wrote that "ladies walk the streets with perfect confidence and security, and the public squares are filled with children at play."[14]

Some Savannah women could be very resourceful. One whom Sherman remembered as Josephine Goodwin told him that with a barrel of flour and some sugar, given to her by the commissary, she had baked cakes and pies that she then sold to the soldiers. Her profit was $56.00. Frances Howard recorded in her diary that she and her friends had persuaded a Union officer to allow the women to feed some 200 hungry Confederate prisoners who were brought into the city on the evening of December 22.[15]

News of the Confederate disaster in Tennessee, however, could only dampen Southern spirits. George Thomas had defeated John Bell Hood at Nashville in mid-December, and prospects could not have looked worse for the future of the Confederacy. "We learn here of General Hood's defeat," a Northern soldier wrote from Savannah. "He made nothing by his northern raid, but lost much." A Richmond correspondent admitted that despair permeated even the Southern capital. Savannah had surrendered; Union soldiers threatened southwestern Virginia; and Hood had "been whipped."[16]

Not everyone agreed that Savannah was returning to normality. It was hard to ignore the presence of the thousands of Union soldiers camped everywhere. Wooden huts and tents blanketed Savannah's squares, and Union vessels docked at the port in ever increasing numbers. An observer who described the city as in the "most dilapidated and miserable condition" claimed that businesses had not reopened, that people remained inside their homes, that fences, sidewalks, and wharves were in disrepair, and that dead horses lay in "the streets by the dozen." One woman was bitterly "surprised to see what these wretches had done in the way of making themselves comfortable. All of our Squares built up with wooden houses so that I scarcely recognized the streets." Yet a Connecticut soldier noted on January 4: "I saw today the stores are beginning to open, so the city looks a little more business like. Last week not a store was open in the city. . . . Now when the harbor is open to the world Savannah must resume its usual commercial position again."[17]

At the same time, Savannah's Unionists took matters into their hands. Not long after Christmas they asked Governor Brown to call a convention to discuss ending the war, and many residents of nearby counties agreed. The group pointed out that with no one left to defend the state except old men and boys, "we think the time has come when our authorities should go boldly to work to negotiate a peace before we are entirely ruined." Supporters even suggested a separate peace: "We have," a Georgian announced, "lost the hope." Unionists wanted the war to end before all the white male population was "butchered." A New York soldier told his sister that "the citizens are mostly for the Union, they held a meeting yesterday [December 28] & voted that the city" should return to Federal rule. Before he mailed the letter, however, the man decided to scratch out "mostly," an indication that he may have had second thoughts about the loyalty of the majority of Savannah's civilians.[18]

Throughout the fall, Governor Brown had been forced to deal with increasing civilian discontent. An Athens resident had written him in mid-October that she had eight children, "and we are about to starve." This letter was typical of those he received from October through early 1865. "There is nothing left, positively nothing, for the people to live on," a woman wrote from Washington in November. After Christmas, a Walker County resident told the governor that deserters were stealing "horses, mules, leather, jeans, money and everything they desire." Anarchy reigned, and Brown could do nothing to answer all the calls for help. "Clouds and darkness are all around us," wrote a Liberty County resident. "The hand of the Almighty is laid in sore judgement upon us; we are a desolated & smitten people." Howell Cobb told his wife that the people were "depressed, disaffected, and too many of them disloyal." It was impossible to escape the bands of lawless men roaming the countryside. From south of Savannah a woman wrote on January 7: "Do the annals of civilized—and I may add savage—warfare afford any record of brutality equaled in extent and duration to that which we have suffered, and which has been inflicted on us by the Yankees? For one month our homes and all we possess on earth have been given up to lawless pillage. Officers and men have alike engaged in this work of degradation." In the northern part of the state, too, a Georgian complained that the mountains were "plum full of Cavalry just . . . stealing all the time."[19]

In fact, the actions of Confederate cavalrymen often headed the list of complaints. From north of Atlanta a woman wrote her husband on December 18 that although the Union soldiers had moved south—"The Yank[ees] went on down the country. I am in hope they will stick in the mud and stay"—the "reb soldier[s] and the citizen[s] steal horse[s]. The reb soldier[s] take what they want. If you will come home, I [will] tell you a heap I can't write." Another woman wrote her brother, a soldier in the Confederate army, "I am sorry to have to tell you so but I must say that I believe we have as mean soldiers as Yankees could be. But don't think by my saying this that I am anyways in favor of the Yankees. . . . But our soldiers have treated us nearly as badly."[20]

Farther up the coast, in Virginia, Georgia soldiers wondered what was happening at home. In late November a soldier had written his wife: "Our news from Georgia is meagre and entirely unsatisfactory. The newspapers publish nothing at all scarcely." On December 17 a man in the Army of Northern Virginia wrote: "I am very much afraid the Yankees paid you a visit. . . . I am afraid to hear from home. I fear I shall hear some bad news perhaps that you have been visited by the Yanks and perhaps all you have destroyed by those scoundrels or perhaps you may be in the army, enduring all the hardships and privations of a soldier." Earlier in the spring one young Georgian confided to his cousin that most Georgians wanted to come home. He had told his future wife, "I don't like this way fighting here in Virginia and letting the yankees run all over Georgia. I had rather fight for those that I love."[21]

Numerous letters reflect the concern of men in Virginia for their families in Georgia. One soldier told his wife on November 28: "My dear, I am very uneasy about you. I ought to have received a letter from you three or four nights ago, but still I hear nothing." He knew that Sherman was somewhere in Georgia, but he added: "I hope things will soon get quiet in that department and Sherman and all

of his army be captured but that is almost one of the impossibili-
ties. To capture as large an army as he has unless we can muster up
a powerful force. They are going to do a great deal of damage unless they are stopped and that right soon. He has already done more
than we can replace in ten years." He assured his wife that he did
not think the soldiers would "try to hurt you or insult you, unless
you should say something out of the way," and concluded, as prag-
matically as possible, "It looks like a dark hour with us, but I guess
it is all for the best, [for] if it is not certainly the all-wise Creator
never would allow it." Another anxious Georgian tried to assure
his wife in December that Sherman would bypass their home: "Your
letter is the latest that I have heard of that did come through. I
suppose it got to Augusta before Sherman cut the railroad. I feel in
great hopes now that no yankees will invade our county. I have
eagerly gathered all the news from Ga I could to find out Sherman's
course. We get nothing scarcely but rumors but from all I can learn
he is making his course east of Macon, and I hope, as I said before,
that he will pass our section unmolested."[22] When news of Sherman's campaign reached the soldiers, Lee worried about deserters
and reduced furloughs to Georgia.

Sherman had trouble with his own army when units from a
black regiment, the 110th U.S. Colored Troops, arrived in Savannah. He ordered the men disarmed and put them to work as laborers, teamsters, and servants. Reports even surfaced that some were
killed by white troops. One Ohio soldier judged that the blacks
needed to be "taught to know their places & behave civilly." Halleck
bluntly told the general that if such behavior toward the 110th continued, he would have trouble with Washington. Although
Sherman's attitude regarding blacks in combat did not change, the
black soldiers in Union blue did accompany the army on its march
through South Carolina.[23]

In preparing for his next step, Sherman told Caroline Petigru
Carson, a South Carolina acquaintance from before the war: "Gladly
will I try to temper the harsh acts of war, with mercy towards those
who by falsehood and treachery have been led step by step from
the generous practice of hospitality to deeds of crime & violence.
. . . I pledge you that my study is to accomplish Peace and honor at
as small a cost to life and property as possible." To Petigru, who
had moved to New York City in 1860 because of her Northern sym-
pathies, he added: "I thank you for the expressions of confidence
in me, and repeat that you do me but justice in thinking that I am

not the scourge and monster that the Southern Press represents me, but that I will take infinitely more delight in curing the wounds made by war, than in inflicting them." As if in a final warning to the Rebels, he closed: "Carolina herself tormented us with posturing and cowardice, and forced us to the Contest. Let her admit her error, and we will soon make all sunshine and happiness, where Gloom and misery reign Supreme."[24]

NOTES

1. Upson, *With Sherman to the Sea*, 145; Sherman, *Sherman's Civil War*, 806.
2. Carlin, *Memoirs*, 160; Cram, *Soldiering with Sherman*, 156–57.
3. John Gourlie to "Dear Brother," December 19, 1864; excerpt from "Foragin With Sherman" by William L. Brower and Freeda Craig Brower, both in Civil War Misc. Collection, USAMHI.
4. Mary E. Hopkins to Thomas W. Bartlett, December 23, 1864, Blanton Family Papers (commas and capitalization have been added to make this excerpt readable); Spencer B. King Jr., ed., "Fanny Cohen's Journal of Sherman's Occupation of Savannah," *Georgia Historical Quarterly* 41 (December 1957): 412.
5. Sherman, *Memoirs*, 2:231; *O.R.* 44, 783; *New York Herald*, December 22 and 27, 1864.
6. *O.R.* 44, 809.
7. Hitchcock, *Marching with Sherman*, 199; Frances Thomas Howard, "Do You Wish to Be Introduced to General Sherman?" in Jones, *When Sherman Came*, 89.
8. Sherman, *Sherman's Civil War*, 778; *Savannah Republican*, December 29, 1864.
9. Sherman, *Sherman's Civil War*, 778.
10. Fellman, *Citizen Sherman*, 164; Marszalek, *Sherman*, 315.
11. Howard, "Do You Wish to Be Introduced to General Sherman?" 90; Sherman, *Memoirs*, 2:234–36; Sherman, *Sherman's Civil War*, 778.
12. Entries dated January 12 and March 18, 1865, Gordon Diary; William W. Gordon to Eleanor K. Gordon, January 14, 1865, all quoted in Anastatia Sims, "Union Torn Asunder: Love and Marriage in Confederate Savannah," paper presented at the conference "Families at War: Loyalty and Conflict in the Civil War South," University of Richmond, April 24–25, 1998; see also Carlin, *Memoirs*, 163.
13. Quoted in Sims, "Union Torn Asunder." One of the three children was Juliette Gordon, who would become Juliette Gordon Low, founder of the Girl Scouts.
14. Sherman, *Sherman's Civil War*, 792; Nichols, *Story of the Great March*, 108.
15. Sherman, *Memoirs*, 2:237; Howard, "Do You Wish to Be Introduced to General Sherman?" 87–88.
16. Osborn, *The Fiery Trail*, 75; *Charleston Mercury*, December 28, 1864.
17. King, "Fanny Cohen's Journal," 414; Miles, *To the Sea*, 238; Russell and Hines, *Savannah*, 125; letter dated January 4, 1864, in Padgett, "With Sherman through Georgia," 63.

18. Joseph Howard Parks, *Joseph E. Brown of Georgia* (Baton Rouge: Louisiana State University Press, 1977), 315; John Gourlie to "Dear Sister Marie," December 29, 1864.

19. Lane, *Times That Prove People's Principles*, 231, 233, 235; Myers, *Children of Pride*, 1242, 1244; T. Conn Bryan, *Confederate Georgia* (Athens: University of Georgia Press, 1953), 153–54.

20. Lane, *Times that Prove People's Principles*, 190, 208.

21. Lane, "*Dear Mother*," 336–38; fragment of letters of William F. Chancelly, dated June 8 and June 19, 1864, typescripts in possession of the author, courtesy of Amma C. Crum.

22. Lane, "*Dear Mother*," 337–38; Marion Hill Fitzpatrick, *Letters to Amanda: The Civil War Letters of Marion Hill Fitzpatrick, Army of Northern Virginia*, eds. Jeffrey C. Lowe and Sam Hodges (Macon: Mercer University Press, 1998), 187.

23. Fellman, *Citizen Sherman*, 163; Glatthaar, *March to the Sea*, 57; Sherman, *Memoirs*, 2:248. The 110th U.S. Colored Troops had been organized at Pulaski in November 1863 as the Second Alabama Colored Infantry; its designation was changed on June 25, 1864. *O.R.* 47, pt. 1, 48, 69, 238.

24. Sherman, *Sherman's Civil War*, 803.

"A GRAND INNOVATOR"
Sherman and Total War

SHERMAN'S VIEW OF SAVANNAH in late 1864 mirrored the positive impressions of Lieutenant John C. Tidball in 1849. "The city of Savannah was an old place," Sherman wrote, "and usually accounted a handsome one." The houses were of brick or frame, though not as impressive as those on "Fifth Avenue or the Boulevard Haussmann of Paris," and the surrounding tropical foliage added an exotic air: the "large yards [were] ornamented with shrubbery and flowers," the street and parks "lined with the handsomest shade-trees of which I have knowledge, viz., the willow-leaf live-oak, evergreens of exquisite beauty; and these certainly entitled Savannah to its reputation as a handsome town." Forsyth Park in particular attracted his notice, "a large park, with a fountain, and between it and the court-house was a handsome monument, erected to the memory of Count Pulaski, who fell in 1779 in the assault made on the city at the time it was held by the English during the Revolutionary War." Outside the city, Bonaventure Cemetery drew the general's praise, as did the "majestic live-oak trees, covered with gray and funereal moss, which were truly sublime in grandeur." Yet of the Savannahians and other Confederates, he wrote that his aim had been "to whip the rebels, to humble their pride, to follow them to their inmost recesses, and make them fear and dread us." As Sherman quoted favorably, "Fear of the Lord is the beginning of wisdom."[1]

In his memoirs, private letters, and official correspondence, Sherman was outspoken about his own significance to the war. After the successful Tennessee and Georgia campaigns he wrote his wife that the decision to divide his army, "with one part to take Savannah and the other to meet Hood in Tennessee [was] all clearly mine, and will survive us both in history." Sherman understood that if his career had ended with the surrender of Atlanta, he would have made but a limited mark on the historical record, for he would have captured a military objective while executing his orders from the

War Department. It was the march to the sea and beyond, something that he alone had envisioned, that burned his name into the nation's memory.[2]

Just before he left Savannah for South Carolina in February, Sherman explained the magnitude of his undertaking. He told Ellen's brother Phil Ewing that he found himself "on the Edge of civilization about to cut loose to attempt another of those Grand Schemes of War that make me stand out as a Grand Innovator. Of course I know . . . that I have done nothing wonderful or new, but only incur risks proportioned to the ability to provide for them." With his knowledge of history, he added: "The Dutch & Greek navigators clung to the Land, but others struck out across the ocean depending on the Compass, and now who clings to the land is deemed the less safe Sailor. So in War, who clings to a base or defends it is less at Ease than one who makes his army strong and don't dissipate it by detachments." Moreover, he knew his name would go down in history: "But let the world draw its own conclusions. I know my Enemy and think I have made him feel Effects of war, that he did not expect, and he now Sees how the Power of the United States can reach him in his innermost recesses."[3]

One of Sherman's biographers wrote, "If it requires great moral courage under such gloomy conditions to launch an army to an attack from a secure base, how much greater the effort and strength of will required to launch an army 'into the blue' knowing that the nearest point, Savannah, where he could hope to secure touch with his own side, was 300 miles distant." A general with Sherman who later chronicled the campaign concluded, "The cool-headed, practical skill that carries out such a plan . . . is only possible to one who unites physical hardihood to mental grasp and unbending will." President Davis admitted that the march "produced a bad effect on our people." General Jacob Cox wrote of the campaign, "The brilliancy of its design and the immense results which followed, have captivated the popular imagination and deeply impressed students of military history everywhere." One unimpressed Union general, however, argued that "Sherman's enormous waste [in Georgia] did not win any battle or cripple any army, and it is doubtful if it shortened the war one day."[4]

At the time of the Savannah campaign, Northern military commanders had worried that if Thomas did not take care of Hood at Nashville, Sherman's march would indeed be remembered as a great mistake. From Virginia, General George G. Meade wrote his wife: "I think it was expected Sherman's movement would draw Hood back to Georgia, but I anticipated just what he appears to be doing—a bold push for Kentucky, which if he succeeds in, will far out-balance any success that Sherman may have in going from Atlanta to the sea coast. . . . I trust old Thomas will come out all right, but the news is calculated to create anxiety." Sherman had strained the rules of war, for the old military maxim is that a commander's true objective is the hostile army on the field and not a geographic site such as Savannah—particularly if that meant abandoning the enemy. Moreover, it could be argued, that unlike Hood, Sherman lacked audacity; he consistently avoided risks.[5]

Among twentieth-century writers, B. H. Liddell Hart, who published his biography of the general in 1929, saw Sherman as "the most original genius of the American Civil War." A British veteran of World War I, Liddell Hart thought it strange that Sherman had not been studied by generals in the Great War. Sherman's next biographer, Lloyd Lewis, who published his book just three years after Liddell Hart's, also praised Sherman for his foresight.[6]

To his advocates, Sherman had a profound effect on future strategy and tactics. "The proper strategy," concluded one individual, "consists in the first place in inflicting as telling blows as possible upon the enemy's army, and then in causing the inhabitants so much suffering that they must long for peace, and force their government to demand it." Many books about the Civil War appeared during the centennial of the 1960s, just sixteen years or so after the end of World War II, the most catastrophic war in world history. Most of those books' authors had been profoundly affected by what they had seen in Europe and the Pacific. Influenced by twentieth-century destruction, they viewed the Civil War as a milestone, a period that ushered in the dawn of total war.[7]

The expression "total war," first used by Giulio Douhet in 1921 after the Great War had left unspeakable carnage, is typically utilized to describe the destruction of resources, both civilian and military, in Germany and Japan during World War II. Civil War historians did not adopt the phrase until after the Second World War.

The first time that Sherman's name was associated with the term was just three years after the end of World War II, when historian John B. Walters published an article in the *Journal of Southern History* titled "General William T. Sherman and Total War." The concept took hold, and soon other historians were analyzing the Civil

War in the same light. This new generation of academics, influenced by events in the first half of the twentieth century, argued
that the Civil War had become "a total war rather than a limited
one."[8] Walters's subsequent book, *Merchant of Terror: General
Sherman and Total War* (1973), is well summarized by its title. It criticized Sherman for his actions against women and children and compared the general to the Japanese and Germans in World War II.
Pursuing this approach, other authors tried to analyze Sherman's
personality and explain his thinking, particularly about war. The
most notable are James M. Merrill in his biography *William Tecumseh
Sherman* (1971); Charles Edmund Vetter in *Sherman: Merchant of Terror, Advocate of Peace* (1992); John Marszalek in *Sherman: A Soldier's
Passion for Order* (1993); Michael Fellman in *Citizen Sherman: A Life
of William T. Sherman* (1995); Stanley P. Hirshson in *The White
Tecumseh: A Biography of General William T. Sherman* (1997); and Lee
Kennett in *Sherman: A Soldier's Life* (2001).[9]

In twentieth-century usage, total war follows a logical course
from the killing of soldiers to the killing of those who provide weapons for the soldier, then on to the reducing of the efficiency of the
enemy's war machine, including the incidental destruction of property, and, if necessary, the killing of civilians, even women and children. Jefferson Davis began to charge the North with atrocities on
the eve of the First Battle of Bull Run (Manassas), and he continued
to make those charges long after the war ended. Because incidents
involving civilians were a cause of bitter debate from the very outset, many students of warfare argued that the North had moved
from traditional war to total war before the conflict ended. Even
so, not all military historians concur that the Civil War can be called
a total war.

Without doubt, Robert E. Lee fought a different kind of war
from that waged by Grant, Sherman, and other Union generals. In
fact, the Union's General John Pope authorized extreme actions in
Virginia in 1862; and no one would disagree that Lee despised Pope
because he included Virginia's civilian population among his military targets. One historian concluded that Sherman benefited "enor-
mously from the fact that a precedent for waging [total] war had
already been set, the legal machinery erected, and the philosophy
accepted" by the time he marched across Georgia and South Carolina. Historian James M. McPherson agrees that in 1862 there was a
"decisive turn toward total war."[10]

There is no doubt that the concept of unrestricted war was one that Union generals such as Sheridan and Sherman advocated. Sherman even told Ellen in June 1864 that all "retire before us, and desolation is behind. To realize what war is one should follow our tracks." And Henry Hitchcock, a member of Sherman's staff, told his wife, "General Sherman is perfectly right,—the only possible way to end this unhappy and dreadful conflict . . . is to make it *terrible beyond endurance.*" A Connecticut soldier who remarked, "I rather felt sorry for some women who cried & begged so piteously for the soldiers to leave them a little" went so far as to add "yet after all I don't know but extermination is our only means now. They feel the effect of this wickedness & who can sympathize very much with them."[11]

Sherman had already used harsh methods to subdue civilians. At Memphis early in 1862 he had threatened to expel women "whose husbands and brothers" fired on Union shipping along the Mississippi River. When he announced he would expel ten families for each boat ambushed, the attacks temporarily stopped. When they resumed, he had a Union regiment destroy all the houses, farms, and crops in a 15-mile-wide sweep along the river south of Memphis. He had begun to see a need to punish the people, not just defeat an army. This attitude matured in 1863, and he wrote in September that his duty was not "to build up, [but] to destroy both the rebel army and whatever of wealth or property it has founded its boasted strength upon."[12]

Moreover, this concept was not unique to Sherman. Thomas Ewing Jr., his foster brother and brother-in-law, was well known for his decision to depopulate several counties in Missouri in an effort to combat guerrillas. With his famous General Orders No. 11, he removed women and children from their homes, the ultimate result being that some were killed in a terrible accident while imprisoned. Yet such events were rare, particularly in the East. Warfare against civilians was more common along the Mississippi River and in the Trans-Mississippi. Missouri and Kansas continued to suffer from the violence that had begun there in the 1850s. In Virginia the armies generally waged war within the parameters acceptable to nineteenth-century Americans. When Sherman marched across Georgia, most people expected him to stay within those unspoken boundaries. But when he said that he would make Southerners feel "the hard hand of war" or that he wanted to "sally forth to ruin Georgia," he sounded like a ruthless warlord. Certainly in his correspondence Sherman used a rhetoric that supports a twentieth-century argument that he advocated total war. In early 1864 he promised "patience and forbearance" to Southerners who acquiesced to his rule, but to anyone who did not, "death is mercy, and the quicker he or she is disposed of the better."[13]

Following the war he became well known for saying "War is hell." Sometimes he denied ever making that comment; at other times he was vague about it, but he certainly made similar statements during and after the war. He even told the West Point graduating class more than a decade after the fighting ended that America was "born in war, baptized in war" and had fought "wars of aggression and defence." Moreover, he said, war was "only the means to an end, to be judged by the motives and the events like other human actions," and it struck the "just and unjust alike." To many Americans, and particularly those Southerners in his path, his march through Georgia and South Carolina was an example of a new kind of war. Remarks such as "war and individual ruin are synonymous terms" only bolstered the argument that he was the father of total war. He was certainly a precursor of the concept that war is not won by armies alone.[14]

Nor would anyone deny that Sherman understood what total war meant, even though that phrase was not used in his time. He certainly understood it during the army's campaigns against the Plains Indians following the Civil War; he showed no sympathy for Native American women or children. Some historians, however, argue that the lack of complete devastation in Georgia points to a "directed" rather than absolute violence against civilians and did not constitute total war. Even some Georgians tried to vindicate Sherman. A woman in Louisville, a town visited by Sherman's armies, wrote following World War I: "When the great War broke out in 1914 and I read of the horrors of the German invasion I made up my mind then that when I go over to live in the other country I am going to hunt up General Sherman and thank him for treating us as kindly as he did."[15]

A Georgia folklorist who studies the stories surrounding Sherman's march compared the general's actions to a devastating campaign in the fight for Welsh independence in the early fifteenth century. Unlike stories of the devastation left in the wake of the fighting between the Welsh and the English, tales surrounding Sherman's march are filled with the names of places he spared.[16]

To a folklorist, what is important is not necessarily what happened but what people perceive as having happened. For example, stories abound, not necessarily true, that Sherman spared a town because he spent the night at the home of a West Point classmate (Covington) or because of an old flame (Madison, Augusta, Savannah) or because the town was just too beautiful to torch (Social Circle, Madison, Savannah). There is even a tale in Madison that local women saved their homes by cooking for Sherman's men. In Jenkinsville, the story goes, Sherman's soldiers took the wood from the church for campfires but spared the town because they had desecrated the church.[17]

Factual or not, these stories indicate that though Sherman knew how to wage unrestricted warfare, he had no intention of treating Southern women and children as he later handled Indian tribes in the West. He never considered slaughter as a means to an end during the Civil War. Rather, one historian has argued, Sherman's concept of total war was only whatever means were necessary to restore "rightful order to the nation," to create a "common cause among the American people," and to forge "spiritual unity" in Northerners and Southerners.[18]

Military theorist Carl von Clausewitz, who died in 1831 and would later be considered the prophet of modern war (although Civil War generals did not study him), wrote that war had three principles: "To conquer and destroy the armed power of the enemy; To take possession of his material and other sources of strength; and To gain public opinion." To accomplish the second, an army must direct "operations against the places where most of the resources are concentrated: principal cities, storehouses, and large fortresses," but public opinion was "won through great victories and the occupation of the enemy's capital. Suppose the country suffers greatly from this," Clausewitz added, "no lasting disadvantage will arise; for the greater the effort, the sooner the suffering will cease." He also declared that victory consisted of bending the enemy to accept your will.[19]

Intuitively, Sherman followed these principles. Battles were not always as important as the intimidation of the civilian population. Even so, what Sherman brought to Georgia's civilian population cannot compare with later events such as the firebombs dropped on people in the cities of Hamburg, Dresden, and Tokyo in World War II. Sherman's march does not even rival many events in previous European wars or such principles as Napoleon wrote in 1812 concerning the occupation of conquered territory: "All persons who have committed excesses, and stirred up rebellion, must be brought before a military tribunal and instantly shot. . . . Get rid of all the prominent men; punish the smallest fault with severity. . . . Hostages are one of the most effective ways to . . . keep conquered provinces under control . . . when the people are persuaded that the death of these hostages would be the immediate result of a breach of their loyalty."[20]

For people in middle and southeastern Georgia, however, the march to the sea was a frightening break from any previous experience. One of Sherman's biographers pointed out that "each war has its *spécificité*, as the French say, its own particular dialogue of violence, its greater or lesser distinction between combatant and noncombatant." Although on occasion the Union army had targeted Rebel sympathizers in regions along and west of the Mississippi River, many Georgians, particularly those safe in Savannah, had remained convinced that they were immune from the direct effect of war; therefore *any* violence was frightening, real or rumored— nonetheless, Brigadier General William P. Carlin claimed, "I can solemnly declare that I never knew any officer or man belonging to my command (First Division, Fourteenth Corps) to participate in setting fire to any residence or other building of any description (except railroads and buildings appertaining to them) on the march of Sherman's army through Georgia or the Carolinas."[21]

What Lincoln authorized, and men like Sherman carried out, was a plan to exhaust Confederate resources and destroy civilian morale. The war had a natural progression: the fighting began in a gentlemanly fashion; it ended in carnage and bloodshed. Historian Lee Kennett noted that Sherman was only "swimming with the tide in a general evolution of policy that would bring to enemy civilians in the army's path increasing stress, privation, and loss. Yet he and others who led the armies at the end of the conflict would still claim that they had not gone beyond the customary and accepted rules of war of their era."[22]

So the debate goes on. Historians who argued that the American Civil War was a total war point out that it has to be understood in the context of American, not global, history. No one would argue that to Americans of the 1860s the evolution in warfare from 1861 until 1865 was revolutionary. That revolution saw a change to warfare unlike anything civilians had experienced before. The guerrilla fighting in Missouri and Kansas was an example of what war could become if unchecked, for guerrilla wars generate their own grim rules.

Opponents of the total war thesis argue that the American Civil War was limited rather than total. For example, the Confederate government passed a partisan ranger act in 1862 that changed the traditional nature of warfare but repealed it in 1864 when it became clear that this law only condoned random violence.[23] Lincoln authorized a detailed set of laws of war in 1863—General Orders No. 100—which covered a variety of actions, but it was often public opinion that kept the generals in check, and in the North, Lincoln was well aware that British journalists sought out stories of extreme violence and printed morbid details in London papers. The Committee on the Conduct of the War carefully scrutinized acts of violence, particularly those aimed at black soldiers or white civilians.

One authority, Marion B. Lucas, argued that "most current historians answer 'no' to the question, Was the Civil War a 'total war'?" Citing Mark Neely's 1991 article, "Was the Civil War a Total War?" and Mark Grimsley's 1995 book, *The Hard Hand of War: Union Military Policy toward Southern Civilians, 1861–1865*, he concluded: "Any definition of total war must include a collapse of distinction between soldiers and noncombatants. No such breakdown occurred in the Civil War on either side, but when lapses existed, they were soldiers against soldiers rather than soldiers against civilians." As he noted, "Sherman never made war on women, children, or the elderly, and in numerous instances—such as Memphis and Columbia—Sherman took care to provide provisions for civilian populations caught in the crossfire of war."[24] Lee Kennett, in *Marching through Georgia: The Story of Soldiers and Civilians during Sherman's Campaign* (1995), concurs.

More recently, James M. McPherson, previously an advocate of the total war thesis, has admitted that "Sherman lacked the killer instinct. Despite his reputation in the South as a ferocious ogre of vengeance and spoliation, Sherman was actually sparing of the lives of his own soldiers, of the enemy's soldiers, and of civilians," committing "surprisingly little personal violence against the white civilian population compared with what many soldiers through history have done." There were "few rapes and fewer murders." Southerners "suffered less than the European civilian population in the Napoleonic wars, during which it is estimated that twice as many civilians as soldiers lost their lives." Sherman's men destroyed property, whereas the "Allied bombers in World War II also destroyed hundreds of thousands of lives."[25]

Sherman saw what he had done as necessary. Among other things, "my march through Georgia and South Carolina," he wrote his brother-in-law, "besides its specific fruits actually produced a marked Effect on Lees Army, because fathers & sons in his Ranks felt a natural Solicitude about children or relations in the regions through which I had passed with Such relentless Effect." In May 1865 he issued a final order to his armies: "Our work is done, and army enemies no longer defy us . . . . [We] destroyed Atlanta [and] struck boldly across the State of Georgia, severed all the main arteries of life to our enemy, and Christmas found us at Savannah. [Now] the War is over, and our Government stands vindicated before the world by the joint action of the Volunteer Armies of the United States."[26] He had helped reunite the country; people both North and South had become Americans again, sharing both name and nation. Sherman understood the concept of psychological warfare even though the term would have meant nothing to him. To reunite the nation he had waged war against Southern civilians, but within limits, for true total war would have resulted in an irreparable schism.

NOTES

1. Sherman, *Memoirs*, 2:230–31, 249.

2. Sherman, *Sherman's Civil War*, 792.

3. Ibid., 810–11.

4. B. H. Liddell Hart, *Sherman: Soldier, Realist, American* (New York: Dodd, Mead, and Co., 1929), quoted in Burne, *Lee, Grant, and Sherman*, 146–47; Jacob Cox, *The March to the Sea: Franklin and Nashville* (New York: The Blue & the Gray Press, n.d.), 2.

5. George Gordon Meade, *The Life and Letters of George Gordon Meade*, 2 vols. (New York: Charles Scribner's Sons, 1913), 2:250.

6. Liddell Hart, *Sherman*, quoted in Marion B. Lucas, "William Tecumseh Sherman v. the Historians," *Proteus: A Journal of Ideas* 17 (Fall 2000): 16.

7. The "elegant description" of strategy is sometimes attributed to Kaiser Wilhelm in World War I. Burne, *Lee, Grant, and Sherman*, 201.

8. John Bennett Walters, "General William T. Sherman and Total War," *Journal of Southern History* 14 (November 1948): 447–80; James M. McPherson, "Lincoln and the Second American Revolution," in John L. Thomas, ed., *Abraham Lincoln and the American Political Tradition* (Amherst: University of Massachusetts Press, 1986), 148–49, 151, 145–55.

9. John Bennett Walters, *Merchant of Terror: General Sherman and Total War* (Indianapolis: Bobbs-Merrill Co., 1973); James M. Merrill, *William*

Tecumseh Sherman (Chicago: Rand McNally, 1971); Charles Edmund Vetter, *Sherman: Merchant of Terror, Advocate of Peace* (Gretna, LA: Pelican Publishing Co., 1992); Marszalek, *Sherman*; Fellman, *Citizen Sherman*; Stanley P. Hirshson, *White Tecumseh: A Biography of William T. Sherman* (New York: John Wiley & Sons, Inc., 1997); and Lee Kennett, *Sherman: A Soldier's Life* (New York: HarperCollins, 2001).

10. Daniel E. Sutherland, "Abraham Lincoln, John Pope, and the Origins of Total War," *Journal of Military History* 56 (October 1992): 585–86; McPherson, *Battle Cry of Freedom*, 490–510.

11. Sherman, *Sherman's Civil War*, 657; Hitchcock, *Marching with Sherman*, 35; letter dated December 28, 1864, in Padgett, "With Sherman through Georgia," 58.

12. *O.R.* 17, pt. 2, 280–81; Sherman quoted in Stephen E. Bower, "The Theology of the Battlefield: William T. Sherman and the U.S. Civil War," *Journal of Military History* 64 (October 2000): 1020. See also *O.R.* 30, pt. 3, 403.

13. Sherman, *Memoirs*, 2:249; see also Bower, "Theology of the Battlefield," 1021; McPherson, *Battle Cry of Freedom*, 809; and *O.R.* 39, pt. 3, 359.

14. Sherman addressed the graduating class of the U.S. Military Academy, West Point, New York, June 14, 1876; *O.R.* 39, pt. 3, 378.

15. A recent study (October 2000) asserting that the Civil War was total war is Bower, "Theology of the Battlefield," 1029–30; an opposing view is found in Lucas, "William Tecumseh Sherman v. the Historians," 15–22. The woman is quoted in *Louisville* (GA) *News and Farmer*, November 21, 1929 [1919].

16. See Elissa R. Henken, *National Redeemer: Owain Glyndŵr in Welsh Tradition* (Ithaca: Cornell University Press, 1996).

17. Steven N. Koppes, "Folklore: Where Fact Meets Fiction," an interview with folklorist Elissa R. Henken, University of Georgia *Research Reporter* (Spring 2000): 13–15.

18. Bower, "Theology of the Battlefield," 1030.

19. Carl von Clausewitz, *Principles of War* in *Roots of Strategy*, 2 vols. (Harrisburg, PA: Stackpole Books, 1987), 2:349–50. This excerpt is from the ten volumes of his collected works published by his widow between 1832 and 1837. The first three, *Vom Kriege* or "On War," contain the most important part of Clauswitz's work. A new edition of his essay "The Most Important Principles for the Conduct of War" in 1936 introduced him to the German people and he is considered "the spiritual father of the German army."

20. Napoleon Bonaparte, *Napoleon on the Art of War*, ed. Jay Luvaas (New York: Free Press, 1999), 125–26.

21. Kennett, *Sherman*, 351; Carlin, *Memoirs*, 156.

22. Kennett, *Sherman*, 351–52.

23. John Singleton Mosby, a favorite of Robert E. Lee, continued to operate as a partisan in Virginia.

24. Lucas, "William Tecumseh Sherman v. the Historians," 18.

25. James M. McPherson, "Blitzkrieg in Georgia," *New York Review of Books*, November 30, 2000, 37–38.

26. Sherman, *Sherman's Civil War*, 852, 909.

BIBLIOGRAPHICAL ESSAY

Sherman's march to the sea has captured the imagination of Americans because it shows the personal side of war. There is much more to the American Civil War than just the big battles, and one of the best of the books that look at individuals—Sherman and his colorful "bummers" as the victors; the people of Georgia as the vanquished—is Lee Kennett, *Marching through Georgia: The Story of Soldiers and Civilians during Sherman's Campaign* (New York: HarperCollins, 1995). An older but still excellent examination of the Union soldier is Joseph T. Glatthaar, *The March to the Sea and Beyond: Sherman's Troops in the Savannah and Carolinas Campaign* (New York: New York University Press, 1985). One of the better popular accounts remains Burke Davis, *Sherman's March* (1980; reprint, New York: Vintage Books, 1988). For a look at the politics of the march, see Anne J. Bailey, *The Chessboard of War: Sherman and Hood in the Autumn Campaigns of 1864* (Lincoln: University of Nebraska Press, 1999).

There are many firsthand narratives by soldiers in the Union army. One of the most valuable is James A. Connolly, *Three Years in the Army of the Cumberland: The Letters and Diary of Major James A. Connolly*, edited by Paul M. Angle (Bloomington: Indiana University Press, 1959). Others include Henry Hitchcock, *Marching with Sherman: Passages from the Letters and Campaign Diaries of Henry Hitchcock*, edited by M. A. DeWolfe Howe (New Haven: Yale University Press, 1927); Charles W. Wills, *Army Life of an Illinois Soldier* (1906; reprint, Carbondale: Southern Illinois University Press, 1996); Alfred Lacey Hough, *Soldiering in the West: The Civil War Letters of Alfred Lacey Hough*, edited by Robert G. Athearn (Philadelphia: University of Pennsylvania Press, 1957); George Ward Nichols, *The Story of the Great March* (1865; reprint, Williamstown, MA: Corner House Publishers, 1972); Thomas Ward Osborn, *The Fiery Trail: A Union Officer's Account of Sherman's Last Campaigns*, edited by Richard Harwell and Philip N. Racine (Knoxville: University of Tennessee Press, 1986); John W. Geary, *A Politician Goes to War: The Civil War Letters of John White Geary*, edited by William Alan Blair (University Park: Pennsylvania State University Press, 1995); Theodore F.

Upson, *With Sherman to the Sea: The Civil War Letters, Diaries, and Reminiscences of Theodore F. Upson,* edited by Oscar Osburn Winther (1943; reprint, Bloomington: Indiana University Press, 1958); William Passmore Carlin, *The Memoirs of Brigadier General William Passmore Carlin, U.S.A.,* edited by Robert I. Girardi and Nathaniel Cheairs Hughes Jr. (Lincoln: University of Nebraska Press, 1999); George F. Cram, *Soldiering with Sherman: Civil War Letters of George F. Cram,* edited by Jennifer Cain Bohrnstedt (DeKalb: Northern Illinois University Press, 2000); George W. Pepper, *Personal Recollections of Sherman's Campaigns in Georgia and the Carolinas* (Zanesville, OH: O. H. Dunne, 1866; and Robert Knox Sneden, *The Eye of the Storm: A Civil War Odyssey,* edited by Charles F. Bryan Jr. and Nelson D. Lankford (New York: Free Press, 2000). This last book merits additional attention because it also includes newly published watercolor sketches of Andersonville, Camp Lawton, and Savannah. For Sherman's cavalry, see Samuel J. Martin, *"Kill-Cavalry," Sherman's Merchant of Terror: The Life of Union General Hugh Judson Kilpatrick* (Madison, NJ: Fairleigh Dickinson University Press, 1996). For a version of the Savannah campaign written by a Union general who did not participate (he was in the Nashville campaign in December 1864), see Jacob Cox, *The March to the Sea, Franklin and Nashville* (New York: The Blue & the Gray Press [distributors], n.d.). Cox relies heavily on the pertinent volumes of *The War of the Rebellion: A Compilation of the Official Records of the Union and Confederate Armies,* 128 vols. (Washington, DC: Government Printing Office, 1880–1901). The *O.R,* of course, is essential to students of the Civil War.

There are some firsthand accounts of Georgians; most of them are written by women. See Dolly Lunt Burge, *The Diary of Dolly Lunt Burge, 1848–1879* (Athens: University of Georgia Press, 1997); Anna Maria Green, *The Journal of a Milledgeville Girl, 1861–1867,* edited by James C. Bonner (Athens: University of Georgia Press, 1964; Eliza Frances Andrews, *The War-time Journal of a Georgia Girl, 1864–1865* (1908; reprint, Lincoln: University of Nebraska Press, 1997); and Katharine M. Jones, comp., *When Sherman Came: Southern Women and the "Great March"* (New York: Bobbs-Merrill Co., 1964). Jones collected stories of the march through both Georgia and South Carolina and published them in one volume. For family accounts, see Robert Manson Myers, ed., *The Children of Pride: A True Story of Georgia and the Civil War* (New Haven: Yale University

Press, 1972); and Malcolm Bell Jr., *Major Butler's Legacy: Five Generations of a Slaveholding Family* (Athens: University of Georgia Press, 1987). For the defense of Savannah, see the firsthand account written after the war by Charles C. Jones Jr., *The Siege of Savannah in December, 1864* (Albany, NY: Joel Munsell, 1874).

Recent books on specific topics are also helpful. For my chapter covering the battle at Griswoldville, William Harris Bragg's *Griswoldville* (Macon: Mercer University Press, 2000), was invaluable (as was his help in preparing this manuscript). To get a feel for the "Empire State of the South," see Mary A. DeCredico, *Patriotism for Profit: Georgia's Urban Entrepreneurs and the Confederate War Effort* (Chapel Hill: University of North Carolina Press, 1988). Others include Joseph Howard Parks, *Joseph E. Brown of Georgia* (Baton Rouge: Louisiana State University Press, 1977); and T. Conn Bryan, *Confederate Georgia* (Athens: University of Georgia Press, 1953). Nathaniel Cheairs Hughes Jr. provides a look at Savannah's defender in *General William J. Hardee: Old Reliable* (1965; reprint, Baton Rouge: Louisiana State University Press, 1992).

The experience of blacks in Georgia is recounted in Clarence L. Mohr, *On the Threshold of Freedom: Masters and Slaves in Civil War Georgia* (Athens: University of Georgia Press, 1986); Whittington B. Johnson, *Black Savannah, 1788–1864* (Fayetteville: University of Arkansas Press, 1996); and Adele Logan Alexander, *Ambiguous Lives: Free Women of Color in Rural Georgia, 1789–1879* (Fayetteville: University of Arkansas Press, 1991).

As would be expected, many books focus on Sherman, notably his own *Memoirs of General William T. Sherman*, 2 vols. (1875; reprint, New York: Da Capo Press, 1984). Equally valuable is *Sherman's Civil War: Selected Correspondence of William T. Sherman*, edited by Brooks D. Simpson and Jean V. Berlin (Chapel Hill: University of North Carolina Press, 1999). Recent biographies of the general include Lee Kennett, *Sherman: A Soldier's Life* (New York: HarperCollins, 2001); Stanley P. Hirshson, *The White Tecumseh: A Biography of General William T. Sherman* (New York: John Wiley & Sons, Inc., 1997); John F. Marszalek, *Sherman: A Soldier's Passion for Order* (New York: Free Press, 1993); and Michael Fellman, *Citizen Sherman: A Life of William Tecumseh Sherman* (New York: Random House, 1995). Some older biographies of the general are cited in the Epilogue. Another useful work is Charles Royster, *The Destructive War: William Tecumseh Sherman, Stonewall Jackson, and the Americans*

(New York: Alfred A. Knopf, 1991). Finally, Marion B. Lucas, "William T. Sherman v. the Historians," *Proteus: A Journal of Ideas* 17 (Fall 2000): 17–21, provides a look at various historical interpretations of the general.

INDEX

Acworth, GA, 45
Alabama: in Hood's campaign, 98; militia, 47; in Sherman's strategy, 23, 48–49
Alabama River, 23
Alexandria, LA, 23
Anderson, George W., 9, 103, 105–6
Andersonville, GA, 67, 81; in Hood's plans, 44; prison at, 41; prisoner exchange, 26–27; and Stoneman's raid, 71
Andrews, Eliza, 70, 84
Antietam, battle of, 30, 66, 99
Army of Northern Virginia, 13, 40, 46, 50, 54, 62, 100–111, 125
Army of Tennessee, 11, 29, 37, 41, 44, 50, 62, 117; October raid, 45–49; strength of, 44
Army of the Cumberland, 30
Army of the Tennessee, 30, 104
Arnold, Richard, 13, 88; surrenders Savannah, 113–14
Atlanta, GA, 40, 66–67, 80, 82, 91, 97, 118, 138; Atheneum Theater, 20; Confederates near, 37; in Confederate strategy, 45–46; destruction of, 53, 88; foraging near, 21–23, 31–32, 46–47, 50, 53–54; inflation in, 19; and Johnston, 95; as Marthasville, 18; population of, 18; and prisoner exchange, 26–27; removal of civilians, 25–26; Sherman's campaign for, 12, 60, 99; in Sherman's march strategy, 24, 41, 45–46, 49; as state capital, 70; surrender of, 18, 129; as Terminus, 18; and terrain, 18; Union occupation of, 17–21, 28
Atlanta Daily Intelligencer, 54
Atlantic & Gulf Railroad, 103
Augusta, GA, 12, 37, 44–45, 47, 54–55, 59, 83, 85, 87, 97–99;

Bragg at, 57, 72, 86; Confederate troops at, 86; feints toward, 86; and folklore, 135; population of, 40; Sherman bypasses, 80–81; as state capital, 65
Augusta Powder Works, 40, 47, 72, 80

Badeau, Adam, 19
Baird, Absalom, 30
Ball's Ferry, 83
Banks, Nathaniel P., 23
Barnard, George, 91
Barnum, Henry, 114
Bartow, Francis S., 9–10
Bartow, Louisa, 9
Bass, John, 79
"The Battle Hymn of the Republic," 62
Beaufort, SC, 88
Beauregard, P. G. T., 43–44, 57, 82, 95, 99–100; and Hood's Tennessee campaign, 84, 97–98; meeting with Brown, 48
Bell, John, 39
Bellamy, Mary Ross, 79
Big Shanty, GA, 45
Blacks: as contraband, 61, 94–95; incident at Ebenezer Creek, 91–93; at Milledgeville, 67, 69; as Union soldiers, 59–61, 87, 126; workers in factories, 71
Blackshear, GA, 82
Blair, Frank P., Jr., 30
"The Bonnie Blue Flag," 111
Bragg, Braxton, 48, 55, 57; at Augusta, 72, 86
Brantley, Allen, 69
Breckinridge, John C., 39
Brown, Elizabeth, 67, 74
Brown, John, 67
Brown, Joseph E., 7, 9, 53, 72, 82, 98; aiding civilians expelled from Atlanta, 26; appeals to civilians, 57; background, 39;

145